Slavery 2.0

Slavery 2.0
No Whips, No Chains, Just Choices

Dr. Sherman D. Rivers, PhD

ISBN: 9781708529840
Imprint: Independently published

Dedication

This book is dedicated to anyone who ever found themselves feeling or thinking that there has to be a better way. That feeling is just the beginning… if you allow it to be. It is my hope that you come to understand the nature of the dynamic between the master and the slave, that there is no escaping that dynamic, and that you choose to be the former and not the latter.

Table of Contents

My Journey

I bring you these words of enlightenment and observation having once been a slave. Your reaction to that statement is probably quite similar to the reactions of countless other individuals upon hearing those words come from my lips. Indeed, it almost seems preposterous to consider that a man could be enslaved in this day and age, much less in a country such as the United States of America. To be quite honest, I probably would have had a hard time believing that myself had I not been the one who had been enslaved.

This country has come to be known as a country possessing clear cut values that serve as a beckoning call for immigrants coming in search of a better life. Individual freedom was the call for some causing them to be willing to pay the price of having to be self-reliant. Equality of opportunity was the call for others causing them to be willing to pay the price of competing in a fiercely competitive environment. For others still, the call was that of the American Dream of an opportunity for a better life and a higher standard of living causing them to be willing to pay the price of hard work. I was not called to come to America, I was born here. I was born into an environment that was at the center of the slave trade in America.

The nature of the slave trade in this country is nothing like it had been centuries ago when it was done completely out in the open and was widely accepted as a fact of life. Things are different now. There are things that are done in secrecy. Secret meetings, secret trades, secret communications, etc. There are also other things, that are (oddly enough) done in plain sight. Although they remain out in the open, they have been done in a certain way for so long that they have become invisible. Invisible, meaning they have moved from the realm of being accepted as fact into the realm of unconscious acceptance. Very little, if any, thought is given to these things. They are what the secret things are founded upon.

I was born into slavery so I had never experienced life as a free man. I had heard of such a thing. It always intrigued me. I had also heard that one could gain their freedom if they were willing to do what was necessary and sacrifice whatever needed to be sacrificed when the time came. I wanted this freedom so bad that I could taste it but, at the same time, I was afraid. I had no idea what awaited me in the free world. This, my friend, is what allows the slave trade to, not only survive in modern America, but thrive! I know this may sound a bit outlandish, or even like outright fantasy. I'm also aware that most people find it difficult to connect with any idea or thought without at least some level of proof. This is why, in the following pages, I will go beyond a mere statement of fact and give you the background information that you will need to clearly understand what I am telling you. That starts with understanding the concept of slavery in and of itself.

Some people would simply define slavery as any system in which people were treated as property and could be bought and sold. We should remember still that "slavery" has also been used to refer to a legal state of dependency to someone else. Be sure to remember that as we move forward with this writing.

Slavery Culture

SLAVERY - FROM THE DAWN OF "SOCIETY" AND "OWNERSHIP"

There is evidence of slavery that predates written records, and further evidence that it has existed in many cultures. Dating back to prehistoric times, the domestication of farm animals apparently served as a model for the enslavement of one's fellow man. Along the banks of the Tigris and the Euphrates rivers in Mesopotamia, along the Nile in Egypt, within the Indus Valley of India, and along the Yangtze River Valley in China were some of the world's oldest known civilizations. Each of these ancient civilizations were known to practice slavery in some form. This was even documented in ancient laws like the Code of Hammurabi showing recognition of and even the administration of the practice. Although the size and scope of the institution appears to have not been as great, this was most likely largely due to the fact that, in times of war, women and children were enslaved as field laborers or concubines while the male captives were most often killed.

It is important to note (before going further) that culture is the sets of social behaviors and norms found in societies. We can dig deeper and see that social behavior is behavior or the range of actions and mannerisms an individual displays in conjunction with themselves or their environment as this takes place between two or more organisms within the same species. As far as norms go, we know that norms are the groups representations of acceptable conduct within that group along with individual perceptions of what is acceptable or not. It's probably a safe bet to say that, in general, people act in a manner that they believe or perceive is acceptable within the culture that they live in and, furthermore, are compelled by society to do so.

How?

Great question!

Within a society, everyday there are new rules put into place, as well as existing rules that may be more structured or that have stood the test of time whether it be for a group or an individual. In addition to just making rules, humans strive to find the rules that come eye to eye with how they perceive that the world works. After being accepted by an individual or a group, those rules then become a norm. Oddly enough, the consequences associated with breaking a rule is really the only difference between a rule and a law. Both have the power to compel a person to do (or go along with) something that they'd rather not.

This is part of the reason that I spent so much of my life as a slave.

I was born into an environment in which those around me were a part of a sweeping current guided by mostly unwritten rules and vaguely understood laws that served to keep me in bondage. I accepted the rules without question. I accepted the laws without understanding. I, initially, accepted my fate as certain. I say "initially" because as time passed and I became more aware of my environment, a desire for something different was kindled inside of me. I didn't understand what it was. I later came to understand that this desire was a desire for freedom. The concept was unclear to me as the culture that I knew all too well was that of a slave culture and not the culture that encourages an enlightened form of free thinking.

So what type of cultures would be required or need to be in place to support slavery as a norm? The consensus over time is that in order for slavery to exist on a large scale, there must be economic surpluses and a high population density. The theory is that slavery would not have existed in "hunter-gatherer" societies but would have lent itself to agricultural societies. Pretty interesting seeing as how, on the surface, that was the divide between the North and the South in the United States right around the time period of the Civil War. An even more important question might be, what type of thinking is required to develop a culture that would support or tolerate slavery as a norm?

Perhaps, the answer lies in the understanding of normative social influences. Social influences can take many varied forms with the effects being manifest in such things as conformity, socialization, peer pressure, obedience, leadership, and persuasion among other things. All of these factors came to bear in creating a culture that not only allowed me to become a slave but to allow countless others to languish in slavery as well. Most of those that I knew when I was held deeply in captivity are still there. I have tried to help them on many occasions but to no avail. Sometimes, the affects of a culture penetrate the individual so deeply that they become powerless to resist even when an opportunity is afforded them. I understand that. And, for that reason, I hold no ill will towards them. They were my friends and family then and they are my friends and family now. The difference is that now I can't remain among them. As a free man, I cannot allow myself to dwell where they dwell although they are welcome to come and dwell with me, should they make an escape and desire to do so.

Slavery Origins

As mentioned previously, there is plenty of evidence that slavery predates the written record and has existed in many different cultures. There is also a ton of well documented evidence of the practice thriving at certain times in recorded history;

Sumer

The earliest known complex society characterized by urban development and social stratification in the historical region of southern Mesopotamia, modern day southern Iraq. Sumer existed during the Copper and early Bronze ages and was situated along the valleys of the Tigris and Euphrates rivers. They were able to grow surplus grains and other crops.

Beneath the king, all members of Sumer society belonged to one of two basic strata: The free person, and the slave.

The Sumerians worshipped hundreds of gods, and it was common for each city to have its own "patron" god. Since the main gods were far too busy and important to worry about the common man, Sumerians essentially picked a minor god or goddess to worship. The expected the deity that they worshipped to interact with the major gods on their behalf. They didn't believe that they would die and go to heaven. They also believed that human goodness had limitations.

The Sumerian view of the gods was that they were above question. For this reason, they easily accepted that the gods were not kind and had every right to do as they pleased regardless of the impact of those decisions on mankind. Each city-state was centered around its temple to the patron god whom they believed owned the city-state. The Sumerians believed that they, along with their slaves, farmed a portion of the land directly for the god. The rest of the land was farmed by either the temple staff or tenant farmers (rent was paid to the temple).

Slaves were an integral part of the Sumerian community. As a result, obtaining slaves was one of the primary objectives of any Sumerian military campaign. In addition to slaves obtained through military conquest, locals could become slaves as well. Usually, this was to satisfy debts. Interestingly, slaves were given the opportunity to do extra work and use the money that they earned to buy their freedom.

It should be noted that the 7 major deities of the Sumerian pantheon; An, Enki, Enlil, Ninhursag, Nanna, Utu, and Inanna were thought of as many to be members of an alien race that created man for one purpose... to be slaves. These gods were called the Annunnaki. The ancient Sumerian myth of Enûma Eliš, inscribed on cuneiform tablets and part of the Library of Ashurbanipal, says humankind was created to serve them. Those who agree with this hypothesis believe that the Annunaki were aliens who came to earth to mine gold for their own uses. According to the Enuma Elish story, the Annunaki created the human race as "hybrid" slaves upon realizing that mining gold was taking a toll on their race.

Ancient Egypt

The first complex society in the region encompassing the northern portion of the African continent. The predictable flooding in the area along with controlled irrigation allowed the Ancient Egyptians to produce surplus crops and allowed for a more dense population. The ancient Egyptians viewed men and women, including people from all social classes except slaves, as essentially equal under the law.

Ancient Egyptians were able to sell themselves and children into slavery as a form of pledge of their services (or family's) as security for the repayment for a debt or other obligation. This "self-sale" of a "free" person into servitude was rarely a choice made by that individuals' free will. Most often, it was the result of individuals being unable to pay off their debts. Sometimes, this arrangement was made out of the need for food, shelter, and clothing. Of course, many were forced into slavery as a result of war and conquest.

For the most part, the majority of slaves in Egypt never really knew if they could ever be free, in this life or the next. An interesting term indicating a specific type of slavery was "Shabti". A Shabti was given the opportunity to have an afterlife. What's more interesting is that as a stipulation of this promise of an afterlife, the slave must obey their master and labor in his service… sound familiar?

Egypt is the setting for the beginning of the origin myth of the Israeli people. This story can be found in the Holy Bible and is spread over the books of Exodus, Leviticus, Numbers, and Deuteronomy. It tale begins with the enslavement of the Israelites in ancient Egypt. It goes on to tell of their liberation through the hand of their God Yahweh, the revelations at biblical Mount Sinai, and then to their subsequent wanderings through the wilderness up to the borders of Canaan, the land their god has promised to them. Essentially, this is the story of people who having been freed from slavery were granted the "god-given" right to murder and subjugate other peoples. Religious belief has often been the basis or excuse for the outright practice of slavery. It can also serve as the basis for slavery in ways that are not so obvious.

Ancient China

Slavery in China dates back to the Shang dynasty when, by some estimates, approximately 5 percent of the population was enslaved. Slaves and human sacrifices were obtained through frequent raids of surrounding states (some believe it was for sacrifice only). During China's warring states period, slavery was practically replaced with the feudal system of landlords and peasants. This brought with it a system of taxation on private land.

Slavery being hereditary can be traced back to as far as the Xia and Shang dynasty (20th - 11th century BCE). Xia and Shang China were based on a social system that closely resembled the system of a slaveholder society. This was in contrast to the feudal society that followed. From China, the concept of slavery apparently quickly spread to neighboring countries like Korea, India, and other Asian lands. There is no mention of the term "slave" (nu 铱) in oracle texts that were written during this time. Just like other ancient civilizations, Shang China introduced slavery to the economy by allowing debtors to repay their debts with women and children. Notice how the human life is reduced to a monetary equivalent. Of note, the Chinese system differed from those of ancient Rome and the Western medieval world because most slaves in China were owned by the state rather than belonging to individuals.

Zhou society showed aspects of both slaveholder and feudal society. The kings of this period gave their followers feudal land, and yet a large part of the population were slaves. These slaves were enslaved as a result of either war or debt and sold in the market. Words describing the concept include characters with multiple meanings, such as "servitude", "punishment", and "dependent on the master". Similarly to what was done by plantation owners in America, powerful feudal lords in ancient China exploited slaves in order to raise production surpluses and gain more wealth. The slaves of China were traded in markets in bazaars of large towns. These were the same places where various other commodities such as silk and cattle were bought and sold.

Arab traders brought East African slaves for what is thought to be the first time during Tang China. In 651 Arab delegates were sent to the Chinese court. This marked the first official contact between the Arab caliphate and Tang Chinese government. By the ninth century the Arabs had established a fairly large community in Guanzhou, and local inhabitants would have been able to see African slaves in Arab households and on trading ships. Some of the wealthy Chinese owned African slaves themselves, whom they kept as doormen. The term for such black people was "Kunlun". Initially, this word first applied to the dark-skinned Chinese. Over time, the meaning of the term grew to have multiple meanings, all of which referred to an individual with dark skin. The Kunlun is mentioned in many stories of fiction written during the Tang dynasty. Many of them describe the Kunlun as having supernatural powers. A famous romance novel in China is "The Kunlun Slave", written in 880 CE by Pei Xing, which stars a faithful Kunlun who uses his supernatural powers to rescue his master's lover from a harem of a high ranking official.

The Kunlun Nu

This fictional account takes place during the Dali reign era (766-80) of Emperor Daizong. It tells the tale of a young man named Cui who enlists the aide of his black slave, Mo-le to help free his beloved who had been forced to join the harem of a court official. According to the story, at midnight, Mo-le kills the guard dogs around the compound and carries Cui on his back while easily jumping to the tops of walls and bounding from roof to roof. Upon reuniting the lovers, Mo-le leaps over ten tall walls with both of them on his back. Cui and his beloved are able to live happily together in peace because the official believes she was kidnapped by knights-errant and did not want to make trouble for himself by pursuing them. In a strange twist of events, two years later, one of the official's attendants sees the girl in the city and reports back to the official. The official arrests Cui and, upon hearing the entire story, sends men to capture the powerful black slave. But, Mo-le escapes with his dagger (apparently his only possession) and flies over the city walls to escape being captured. He is seen over ten years later selling medicine in the city, not having aged a single day.

The story of the Kunlun slave is interesting in that it seems to suggest an acknowledgement of the physical prowess of the black slave. It also suggests that the darker skinned people seemed to age better and not show the signs of aging in the same manner as the local population.

Ancient Greece

Slavery was a common practice in great history from the around the 12th - 9th centuries BC until around 600 AD.

Some Ancient Greek writers (including, most notably, Aristotle) considered slavery natural and even necessary. This way of thinking was famously questioned in the Socratic dialogues; the first recorded condemnation of slavery was put forth by the Stoics.

In ancient Greece there were four primary sources of slaves: war, in which the defeated would become slaves to the victorious unless a more objective outcome was reached; piracy (at sea); banditry (on land); and international trade. By the rules of war of the period, the victor possessed absolute rights over the vanquished, whether they were soldiers or not and enslavement, while not systematic, was common practice. Piracy and banditry provided a large and consistent supply of slaves. Pirates and brigands would typically demand ransom whenever the status of their catch warranted it. Usually, whenever ransom was not paid or not warranted, they would simply sell the captives to a trafficker. Additionally, there was slave trade between kingdoms and states of the wider region.

An ancient Greek slave of note is Aesop. He is credited with the writing of Aesop's fables although it is not really known if he actually existed at all. The earliest Greek sources of information, including the philosopher Aristotle, suggest that he was born in 620 BCE. Most descriptions of him indicate that he was, if he existed, a very unattractive man by the standards of his time. There is also the question of his possible African origin. A later opinion suggests that he was a black African from Ethiopia.

Ancient India

According to Arthashastra (an ancient Indian treatise on statecraft), anyone who had been found guilty of minor crimes, has been ruined, or is bankrupt may mortgage themself to become "dasa" for someone willing to pay his or her bail and employ the dasa for money and privileges. A form of indentured servitude.

Shamasastry's 1915 foundational translation of the Arthashastra describes the rights of the dasa. The insight given is that they were quite different than slaves in other ancient and medieval civilizations. For example, it was illegal to force a dasa (slave) to do certain types of work, to hurt or abuse him, or to commit rape against a female dasa.

The following rules were found in the translation:

Employing a slave (dasa) to carry the dead or to sweep ordure, urine or the leavings of food; keeping a slave naked; hurting or abusing him; or violating the chastity of a female slave shall cause the forfeiture of the value paid for him or her. Violation of the chastity shall at once earn their liberty for them.

When a master has connection (sex) with a pledged female slave (dasa) against her will, he shall be punished. When a man commits or helps another to commit rape with a female slave pledged to him, he shall not only forfeit the purchase value, but also pay a certain amount of money to her and a fine of twice the amount to the government.

A slave (dasa) shall be entitled to enjoy not only whatever he has earned without prejudice to his master's work, but also the inheritance he has received from his father.

It should be noted that he term dasa in Indic literature can mean slave or servant. It could also be used to refer to a it refers to a religious devotee.

Roman Empire

Slavery played an important role in Roman society as well as its economy. Slaves performed many domestic services (aside from manual labor), and it was common for them to be employed at highly skilled jobs and professions. Even accountants and physicians were often slaves. Slavery was quite different for those who were either unskilled or sentenced to slavery as punishment in that their work was hard, living conditions brutal, and their lives short. Slaves were considered property and not people. Despite this, there were many cases of poor people selling their children into slavery during hard times.

Slaves who attempted escape and were later caught were usually dealt with harshly. The same could be said of the treatment of those who rebelled against their masters as in the case of the captured slaves of the army of Spartacus. Those 6,000 slaves who were taken prisoner were crucified along the Appian Way (the main road into Rome). Their bodies were left to hang on the crosses for several months as a warning to other slaves who might consider the possibility of rebelling against their Roman masters.

Fortunately, not all slaves were treated badly. Historical accounts reveal that an African slave by the name of Terrance, impressed his master so much with his intelligence that the master educated him and later set him free. Ultimately, he became one of Rome's most important writers.Terence was born in Carthage (Africa) in about 190 BC. Terence the African slave wrote six plays: Adelphoe (The Brothers), Andria (The Girl from Andros), Eunuchus, Heauton Timorumenos (The Self-Tormentor), Hecyra (The Mother-in-Law) and Phormio.

Although they were not very popular at the time, Terence is now considered to be one of the most important writers of the Roman Empire. His work was praised by Scipio Aemilianus Africanus and Laelius Gaius but only one of his plays, Eunuchus, enjoyed any success during his lifetime.

The Romans were not the first people to use slaves, but no one in history has relied on them as much as they did. It has been estimated that when the Roman Empire was at its most powerful, two million out of the six million people living in Italy were slaves.

Arab Slave Trade

Early Islamic texts encourage kindness towards slaves and the freeing of one's slaves at some point. It also permitted (if not encouraged) the enslavement of non-Muslim prisoners of war. The North African slave markets traded also in European slaves. The European slaves were acquired by Barbary pirates in slave raids on ships and with raids on coastal towns from Italy to Spain, Portugal, France, England, the Netherlands, and as far off as Iceland. Men, women, and children were captured to such a devastating extent that vast numbers of sea coast towns were abandoned.

A popular figure coming from the Arab slave trade was a man named Tippu Tip. He was believed to have been born around 1832 in Zanzibar. His mother was a Muscat (largest city of Oman) Arab of the ruling class. His father and grandfather were from the coastal area in Southeast Africa inhabited by the Swahili people. His proper name was Muhammad bin Juma bin Rajab el Murjebi. Tippu Tip was a dealer in Ivory and slaves. He was often referred to as Tippu Tib which is translated as , "the gatherer together of wealth".

Through cunning and aggressive action, Tippu Tip built a trading empire. He used the wealth created through the dealing of human cargo, among other things, to found clove plantations on Zanzibar. Abdul Sheriffa Tanzanian Meritus history professor at the University of Dar es Salaam reported that when Tippu Tip left for his twelve years of "empire building" on the mainland, he had no plantations of his own. By 1895, he had acquired "seven 'shambas' (plantations) and 10,000 slaves"

Pre-Columbian Civilizations of the Americas

Allowing individuals to own, buy, and sell other individuals was prevalent among the indigenous people of both North and South America. After the English settlers arrived, five tribes imitated the English and came to own black slaves. European colonies purchased indigenous peoples as slaves. It has been estimated that between two and five million indigenous people were enslaved as part of this trade. Slavery is illegal throughout the Americas yet some indigenous people remain slaves in every way but name.

Slavery of Native Americans was illegal in Spain or Spanish territories. However, slavery in other contexts as an institution still existed in Spain itself, among them were Ottoman and Barbary prisoners and Muslim rebels from southern Spain following the Reconquista. Isabella and Ferdinand rejected Columbus' enthusiasm for the slave trade. They issued a decree in 1500 which specifically forbade enslavement of natives, but there were three exceptions which were freely used by colonial Spanish authorities to evade the prohibition: cannibals (Caribs, one target population, practiced ceremonial cannibalism); those taken in "just wars"; and slaves purchased from other indigenous people.

Slave labor was first used to mine the gold deposits of Cibao on Hispaniola. After the natives of Hispaniola were worked to death using the system that rewarded conquerors with the labor of the vanquished, the other islands of the Caribbean were scoured for slaves. A shortage of labor resulting from a smallpox epidemic in 1518 resulted in an intensified search. By 1521 the islands of the northern Caribbean, such as the Bahamas inhabited by the peaceful Taino people, were for the most part depopulated.

The pearl fisheries on the coast of Venezuela was another activity which had a high attrition rate. The divers were locked in their quarters at night by the Spaniards. The Spanish believed that if the divers (who were mostly male) had sex, they would not be able to submerge but rather would float on the water. The divers who either had a small catch or rebelled were beaten with whips and tied in shackles. Long working days and injuries could affect the health of many of the divers. In addition, the coastal waters were often infested with sharks, so shark attacks were common. Eventually, the Spaniards began to import African slaves as the indigenous populations died off from disease and over-exploitation. In fact, Africans became so preferred by the Spanish over indigenous labor that a royal decree of 1558 decreed that only Africans (and no natives) should be used for pearl diving.

A Mainstream Practice

A quick glance at some of the aforementioned examples and it becomes pretty safe to say that slavery has been around, if not mainstream, and thriving for quite some time. Do you remember the two conditions that were required to produce a cultural environment that was conducive to slavery? As mentioned earlier, there must be economic surpluses and a high population density. So, moving forward in time, we can see the groundwork that had been laid to produce a culture of slavery in America. It's important to understand its foundations and life cycle in the past in order to understand how and why it still exists in America...in this day and age.

The Story of Spartacus

SPARTACUS ESCAPED SLAVERY AND FORMED AN ARMY

References in history tell us that Spartacus was a gladiator of Thracian descent. There isn't much information about him prior to the point at which he became a slave of the Roman Empire. Some say that he may have been a soldier in the Roman Army while others argue he was fighting for an opposing army and was captured. The prevailing belief is that he was a Roman deserter who was captured and forced into slavery.

A rebellion in 73 BC at the gladiatorial training school at Capua has been interpreted by some (and rightfully so) as an example of oppressed people fighting for their freedom against a slave owning power structure controlled by a few people created an opportunity for Spartacus to escape along with about 70 other gladiators. Their numbers grew, bolstered by the addition of other runaway slaves. This growing group based itself at Mount Vesuvius where new arrivals that weren't already skilled at combat were given combat skills training. The leadership of this newly formed military unit included; Spartacus, Crixus, and Oenamus. Crixus and Oenamus were both Gauls (a group of Celtic peoples of West-Central Europe).

As if often the case regarding those in power, Rome didn't take an Army comprised of slaves seriously and didn't send their best troops to meet the threat. As a result, the slave Army made quick work of the first few forces it came up against. More victories saw more slaves joining the slave army's ranks. It was thought that Spartacus wanted to lead this Army over the Alps and into freedom while Crixus want to use this Army to attack Rome and deal a blow to the empire while freeing the large population of slaves and swelling the army's ranks even more. As a result, Crixus (and the forces under his command) splintered off and began attacking various targets along the countryside before being defeated and killed.

Spartacus and the remaining forces continued to engage the Roman forces winning three additional battles before turning south for some unknown reason. Rome now took the slave army seriously and sent an experienced commander, Marcus Crassus, to meet it with battle hardened troops. After a few skirmishes and much pursuit, Marcus Crassus defeated the slave army in southern Italy. It is believed that Spartacus was killed during the final battle but his body was never found.To serve as a warning for others who might rebel against their condition of slavery, around six thousand slaves were crucified with their bodies lining the road between Rome and Capua.

The story of Spartacus reminds us that slavery does not have to be a permanent condition. It reminds us that some will pursue freedom by rising up and entering into direct opposition with their oppressors. It reminds us that some are willing to die in the pursuit of freedom.

Consideration:

Spartacus, having been a free man at one point in his life, if not most of it, was resistant to the idea of being enslaved in the traditional sense. Going from being free to being enslaved was more or less a backward step in the evolution of his life. The practice was common place in that time. A man could lose his freedom in a number of ways. From indebtedness, to a loss in battle, to violating a law in some form, the possibilities were numerous. What's most important is the mindset that is adopted once this occurs. Many people of the day that went through that probably simply resigned themselves to their fate.

The average man who had been turned into a gladiator probably thought that he had two choices when, in reality he had at least three. The first choice, an obvious one, was to simply accept one's fate to die in gladiatorial combat as entertainment for onlookers. A man in this situation might consider suicide as an option. He might chose the leave the game, to exit the game by the only real way out, death. In any case, he will have resigned to himself that he had nothing left to leave for as he would never be free again.

Another type of man might look at the situation a bit differently. Although he has accepted that he has been enslaved and may never be free again, it is clinging to life that is most important for him. In this case, the man takes the second choice and begins to devote himself to the mental and physical toughness necessary to survive as long as he can. For him, survival is life. Each day brings with it another challenge and he must rise to that challenge if he wishes to live. Free or not, life is what is most important.

Then there is the type of man who would take the third choice. The third choice in this situation is decidedly different because this man has not accepted death as the inevitable outcome and he has not accepted slavery as a possible permanent condition. For him, his condition is temporary, unnatural, and not to be tolerated beyond the point in which he has an opportunity (no matter how perilous) to take action to change it. As with the other survival-minded man, he too devotes himself to strengthening his mind and his body. The difference is that he does not do this with merely the intention of surviving, he does this so that he is ready to capitalize on any opportunity that should present itself wherever and however that occurs. Spartacus was a man of the third type. He realized that the condition of slavery was indeed a temporary condition and one that could be rectified. How slim of the chance of freedom was of no consequence to him. What mattered is that a chance existed. It was possible. And when that opportunity presented itself, he seized it.

Religion and Slavery

RELIGION CAN BE NEITHER COMPLETELY BLAMED OR ABSOLVED

Religion, at its core, is simply a set of beliefs that is passionately held by a group of people that is reflected in the way that they see the world. These beliefs are often ritualized. There are many different religions and subsets of them, many of which are not readily identified. Each of these individual, although sometimes very similar, has a different set of beliefs. Each of these beliefs contribute to the attitude we have whenever we take something to be accurate or true creating a belief "system" that guides or influences or decisions and ultimately our lives. We like to think of religion as a higher order of thought promoting good and virtuous ideals of man and connecting him with a godly force. We see virtuous goals. On the other hand, regarding slavery, we see that because goals are based (at least in part) on beliefs, the success or failure at achieving a particular goal may contribute to the development and modification of beliefs that support those goals. In other words, religion is often developed in such a way that it makes allowances for certain behaviors if they are "profitable" or good for the members of the flock. We see evidence of this across the religious spectrum.

Judaism

Judaism is the religion associated with the ethnic group originating from the Israelites and Hebrews of historical Israel and Judah. Jewish ethnicity, nationhood, and religion have a strong relationship with one another. It is an ancient religion It features the belief in the existence of only one god that created the world, is all-powerful, and intervenes in the affairs of man. It is an Abrahamic religion meaning it is comprised of communities of faith that claim descent from the ancient Israelites and the worship of the God of Abraham. The term "Abrahamic" comes from the name of the patriarch Abraham. Judaism is considered one of the oldest monotheistic religions.

The Torah is the foundational text of Judaism. Within the Torah are instructions and direction for the religion, philosophy, and culture of the Jewish people. It is considered (by religious Jews) to be the written expression of the agreement or covenant that God made with the Children of Israel. The Torah is part of a larger text known as the Tanakh or Hebrew Bible which is the canonical (rule or measuring stick) collection of Hebrew scripture.

With between 14.5 and 17.4 million people practicing Judaism worldwide, it is the 10th largest religion in the world.

What does Judaism have to say about slavery?

Judaism's ancient and medieval writings contain many laws regulating bth the ownership and the treatment of slaves. The slavery laws of the Israelites can be found in the Hebrew Bible and are similar to the laws found in the Code of Hammurabi. There are actually two sets of laws governing slavery in the Hebrew Bible; one set governs the treatment of Canaanite slaves. The other set governs the treatment of Hebrew slaves. The laws governing the treatment of Canaanite slaves applied to all non-Hebrew slaves.

In the second through the fifth centuries, the Talmud established a single set of rules for the treatment of all slaves with a few exceptions regarding treatment of Hebrew slaves. Included in these laws was description of punishment prescribed for those slave owners that mistreated their slaves. These were the laws cited by pro-slavery supporters as religious justification for slavery in America.

As far as freeing slaves goes, the Tanakh contains the rule that Jewish slaves would be released following six years of service. Non-Jewish slaves could be potentially enslaved for life.

Islam

Islam, like Judaism, is another religion of Abrahamic origins claiming descent from Abraham. It also features the belief in the existence of only one god that created the world, is all-powerful, and intervenes in the affairs of man. In terms of size and number of followers, Islam is the world's second largest religion boasting over 1.8 billion followers. Twenty-four percent of the world's population are followers of Islam, most commonly known as Muslims. Muslims make up the majority of the population in 50 countries. The primary scriptures in the Muslim religion are viewed as the exact word of God along with the teachings of

Muhammad called the sunnah and contained in a book called the Quran. Muslims believe that Islam is the complete and all encompassing version of the state of purity and innocence that all humans are born with. This is called the "fitra" or "fitrah" meaning " original disposition", "natural constitution", or "innate nature". According to Islamic theology, human beings are born with an innate inclination of rawhide (Oneness), which is contained in the fitra along with compassion, intelligence, insane (excellence) and all other attributes that embody the concept of humanity.

Rather than referring to those who embrace Islam as converts, many Muslims prefer to refer to them as reverts with the belief that these people are merely returning to a "pure state".

What does Islamic history say about slavery?

Although it was not always the case, in practice, Islamic law does not have a racial component, in theory. Slaves, throughout history, could be found in many different types of roles ranging from that of a domestic worker to that of a high ranking government official. This contrast in the positioning of slaves in Islamic society could be seen in the fact that a slave could be a trusted military officer or administrator in one case or, in another case, be a laborer receiving such harsh treatment that it warranted or caused a slave uprising. This was the case regarding the Zanj Rebellion which was a major uprising taking place from the year 869 to the year 883 under the Abbasid central government. Even still, the majority of the labor pool in the

Islamic world during the medieval time period consisted of paid laborers.

The most well known involvement between Islam and slavery is probably the Arab slave trade which was most active in West Asia, North Africa, and Southeast Africa. During this time, Muslim traders were responsible for exporting as many as 17 million slaves to the coast of the Indian Ocean, the Middle East, and North Africa. Barter for slaves occurred primarily between the medieval era and the early 20th century, conducted via slave markets, and with the slaves captured mostly from Africa's interior and Southern Europe.

Some historians believe that as many as 17 million people were sold into slavery on the coast of the Indian Ocean, the Middle East, and North Africa, and about 5 million African slaves were transported by Muslim slave traders via the Red Sea, the Indian Ocean, and the Sahara desert to other parts of the world between 1500 and 1900.

Hinduism

Large bodies of Hindu texts known as Vedas regard liberation to be the ultimate goal in life with is contrary to slavery. Slavery is condemned in the verbally transmitted Hindu texts. There were, of course, people who were employed as laborers on farm lands that fit the definition of slaves in the purist sense in that they could be given away as gifts along with the land on which they worked. Slavery, in Hinduism could come about it different ways; one could become a slave through debt, one could become a slave as a result of being sold into slavery by one's parents, or one could become a slave as punishment for a crime. Different rules applied to different classes of people stating that some could not be subjected to slavery and that the selling or mortgaging of certain classes of enslaved individuals was itself punishable as a crime.

Buddhism

Language regarding slavery could be found in early Buddhist texts such as "the slave cannot become a Bhikkhu". This meant that slaves were forbidden the opportunity to become a Buddhist monk. Other texts mention and show that those who failed to pay their debts were enslaved and the religion did not allow debtors and slaves to join their monasteries.

Christianity

Christianity, another Abrahamic religion is a direct descendant of Judaism (developing during the 1st century) and is based on the life and teachings of Jesus of Nazareth as put forth in the New Testament of the Holy Bible. Those who follow Christianity are known as Christians. Christians believe that Jesus is the Son of God and the savior of mankind. Christianity in the largest religion in the world boasting over 2.4 billion followers. At least 31.5 percent of the world population is Christian. It spread throughout the Roman Empire, Ethiopia, the Caucasus, and Asia during the first centuries of its existence.

The development of Western civilization has been predominately influenced by Christianity, especially in the area of Europe during the classical transition into the middle ages and on into the middle ages. Today, Christianity is still the dominant religion of the west with over 70 percent of the population identifying themselves as Christian. It also continues to grow in Africa and Asia. Basic convictions are shared among Christians around the world but there are different interpretations and opinions regarding the Bible and the sacred traditions upon which Christianity is based.

What are some Christian views on slavery?

Based on material readily available in the New Testament, slavery was a rudimentary element of the social and economic framework. In fact, many of those who became Christians in the early days of the religion were slaves. Treatment of slaves, in Christianity is referenced on numerous occasions in the Bible. The apostle Paul spoke to slaves in his writing;

Slaves, obey your earthly masters with respect and fear, and with sincerity of heart, just as you would obey Christ.
- Ephesians 6:5

And also to the masters;

And masters, treat your slaves in the same way. Do not threaten them, since you know that he who is both their Master and yours is in heaven, and there is no favoritism with him.
- Ephesians 6:9

There have been conflicting views on slavery within the Christian faith since the Middle Ages. For example, the proceeds of slave ownership directly supported the church mission activities in the Caribbean under the terms of a charitable bequest in 1710. In Barbados, two historic sugarcane producing estates owned by the Codrington family (Codrington Plantations) were granted to the Society for the Population of the Gospel in Foreign Parts to fund the establishment of Codrington College. During the early years of ownership by the society, hundreds of slaves were branded on their chests using red hot iron brands with the word "society" putting others on notice that these slaves were owned by the society. Having since apologized for the "sinfulness of our predecessors", the Church of England sets forth an example of the church's inconsistent approach to slavery.

At times, passages in the Bible have been used as justification for the keeping of slaves as well as how that should be done. Many Christians used these passages from the Bible to speak out agains t the abolitionist movement in support of the continuation of slavery. In both Europe and the United States, some Christians were under the belief that the words and doctrines in the Bible actually justified slavery;

[Slavery] was established by decree of Almighty God...it is sanctioned in the Bible, in both Testaments, from Genesis to Revelation...it has existed in all ages, has been found among the people of the highest civilization, and in nations of the highest proficiency in the arts.

- Jefferson Davis, President, Confederate States of America

... the right of holding slaves is clearly established in the Holy Scriptures, both by precept and example.

- Richard Furman, President, South Carolina Baptist Convention

The 20th century opposition to the American Civil Rights Movement had basis in many of the same religious ideas that had been used to justify slavery in the 19th century. Large numbers of Native Americans were enslaved. Slavery under Christian beliefs was not restricted to the continental United States. It's been estimated that for each slave that landed in North America, South America imported around twelve slaves, and the West Indies over ten.

Consideration:

People like to do one of two things when it comes to religion in regards to the bad things that have happened in the past or are happening now; they either blame religion for it having had happen or they absolve religion of any and all responsibility, The truth of the role of religion in the bad happenings of this world is somewhere in between. Religion cannot possibly be blamed for everything bad that has happened. By the same token, religion cannot be absolved of owning at least a portion, if not most, of the responsibility.

Politics and Slavery

POLITICS IS ALL ABOUT WHO GETS WHAT, WHEN, AND HOW...

Slavery 2.0

If you're like most people that I know, slavery in America is the first thing that comes to mind when you hear the word "slavery". Oddly enough, one of the first things that comes to many people's mind when they hear the word "America" is liberty or freedom. Isn't that pretty interesting? What makes it even more interesting is the fact that the words of Francis Scott Key are primarily responsible for the latter thought coming to mind as he wrote "the land of the free and the home of the brave" in 1814. During this time, slavery was alive and kicking in America. Those words have been sung as the national anthem of the United States of America since 1931, during which time segregation and discrimination were rampant across the country. We can see that words, their meanings, and how we relate to them are all about perception and the social status of the individual who is hearing or speaking those words.

I was unaware of the "other side of the coin" when I grew up being taught to sing the national anthem with reverence. As far as I knew, it was a song worthy to be sung loudly and clearly so that all within the sound of it would know the greatness of the United States of America. I wasn't aware of the totality of the lyrics of "The Star Spangled banner" written by Sir Frances Scott Key. I didn't know that there were additional lyrics to the song that I had never heard before.

And where is that band who so vauntingly swore
That the havoc of war and the battle's confusion,
A home and a country, should leave us no more?
Their blood has washed out their foul footsteps' pollution.

No refuge could save the hireling and slave
From the terror of flight, or the gloom of the grave:
And the star-spangled banner in triumph doth wave,
O'er the land of the free and the home of the brave.

The first time that I heard of that, "No refuge could save the hireling and slave" it took me by surprise. I had not realized how the concept of slavery remained deeply embedded in the fabric of not just the United States but the whole world. The American system was simply the best reference that I had to initiate what would later become an expanded view of slavery.

The system in the United States in which property laws applied to people was the legal institution of chattel enslavement. Chattel slavery is sometimes referred to as "traditional slavery" and simply means that people were treated as personal property of the owner and bought and sold as commodities. This primarily involved Africans or those of African decent existing in the good ole USA in the 18th and 19th centuries. This shameful treatment of human beings had been practiced in British America which included the British Empire's colonial territories in North America from 1607 to 1783. Having been legal in all of the Thirteen Colonies during the Declaration of Independence in 1776 it continued on until at least 1865 in that form.

The Thirteenth Amendment, in effect, ended slavery as we traditionally think about it in the United States by making it unconstitutional. The same went for involuntary servitude in which a person was laboring against that person's will for the benefit of another. We'll touch back on this later as well. Of significance, is the fact that slavery and involuntary servitude were not made unconstitutional altogether, the practice was still permissible as punishment for a crime. Penal labor is specifically allowed by the 13th Amendment to the U.S. Constitution in the statement, *"neither slavery nor involuntary servitude, except as a punishment for a crime whereof the party shall have been duly convicted, shall exist within the United States, or any place subject to their jurisdiction."* Interestingly enough, there is no reference to what type of crime. The only requirement for slavery or indentured servitude to be okay is a conviction. So, based on that, one can conclude that slavery is actually still legal in the United States of America.

Do you know anyone (other than me) who has spent part of their life as a slave?

Race had become the basis for institutionalized slavery in America by the time of the American Revolution with that status being associated with African ancestry. This was in spite of the fact that there were free people of color who were voting citizens when the United States constitution was made official in 1789. Following the Revolutionary War, the abolitionist movement gained a foothold in the north and slavery (as most know it) declined in the north due to changes in the laws. Meanwhile, the folks down south were trying to expand the practice. They wanted to spend it into the west as the country expanded.

Here is a thought; why do you think the folks down south were so in favor of not only keeping slavery in place but also expanding the practice?

Easy answer, "King Cotton"

The cotton industry had undergone and was continuing to undergo rapid expansion in the states that were most dependent on plantations and slave societies during the period before the Civil War. It is not uncommon to refer to the region as the cotton states. Cotton was the primary crop that was grown to sell for profit. The cotton gin, a machine that eased and sped the separation of cotton fibers from their seeds, actually increased the need for slave labor rather than reducing it in that demand was increased for labor to pick the cotton when the cotton all ripened at once.

In addition to continuing on as slave societies, southern states and southern democrats wished to extend slavery into the newly obtained western territories with the reasoning that this would help them to maintain their political power in the nation. These same people wanted to take over Cuba making it a slave territory. All of this led to the divisiveness that ultimately led to the Civil War having split the nation into states that were pro-slavery and those that were not. On a map, the separation between the northern (anti-slavery) states and the southern (pro-slavery) states was indicated by a geopolitical border among four states forming part of the borders of Pennsylvania, Maryland, Delaware, and West Virginia known as the Mason-Dixon line.

You could sum up the previous two paragraphs by saying that slavery was simply a means to compel human beings to be the labor force required to earn money or profit. You could further summarize that the PRIMARY reason that slavery went away in the north was that it was no longer necessary (due to the industrial revolution) to grease the wheels of the profit machine. Alternatively, one could also surmise that the PRIMARY motivation for the southern desire to not only uphold but to expand slavery was for the exact opposite reason. Slavery was necessary to grease the wheels of the southern agricultural profit machine. Sure enough, there were many other "reasons" for wanting to either abolish or maintain slavery as a way of life but MONEY and the power that came along with that was hands down the highest motivating factor. Once one gains a true understanding of that, one's mind can begin to grasp more complex concepts in that area of thought and begin to truly understand the nature of slavery.

One testament to the fact that slavery (as most know it) in America was more about profit than it was about race (although a basis for status) was that there were people of African decent who were slaveholders holding others of African decent as slaves. One of these men, Anthony Johnson, even went so far as to sue for ownership of another black man named John Casor. So not only were there cases of negroes owning negroes but there were negroes going to court to own negroes because they wanted to own another negro so bad. It was all about the money, the profit, the capital...human capital...or "human resources" as they like to call it nowadays.

American historian and former president of Phi Beta Kappa John Hope Franklin wrote:

A large majority of profit-oriented free black slaveholders resided in the Lower South. For the most part, they were persons of mixed racial origin, often women who cohabited or were mistresses of white men, or mulatto men ... Provided land and slaves by whites, they owned farms and plantations, worked their hands in the rice, cotton, and sugar fields, and like their white contemporaries were troubled with runaways.

American historian and professor of history wrote:

In slave societies, nearly everyone—free and slave— aspired to enter the slaveholding class, and upon occasion some former slaves rose into slaveholders' ranks. Their acceptance was grudging, as they carried the stigma of bondage in their lineage and, in the case of American slavery, color in their skin.

Henry Louis Gates Jr, African American history and culture scholar wrote:

... the percentage of free black slave owners as the total number of free black heads of families was quite high in several states, namely 43 percent in South Carolina, 40

*percent in Louisiana, 26 percent in Mississippi, 25 percent
in Alabama and 20 percent in Georgia.*

What does this tell us?

It tells us at least two things;

(1) A desire for profit often supersedes the the ideal of
freedom and liberty for EVERY man or woman or child
with a clear disconnect, in terms of humanity, occurring
among those in power or in possession of the resources.

(2) Those who were at one point victims of slavery will
often take no issue with levying that same abuse on
others if given an opportunity or placed in a position to
do so.

In 1808, the Act Prohibiting Importation of Slaves of
1807 went into effect making it illegal for new slaves to be
imported into the United States. Thomas Jefferson was the
President at the time having declared that all men were
created equal while yet owning large numbers of slaves
himself. This act only made it illegal to import new slaves
into America but the slave trade within the country was alive
and well at that time. In fact, the slave trade was actually
protected by the United States Constitution in Article 1 of
Section 9 which stated;

The Migration or Importation of such Persons as any of
the States now existing shall think proper to admit, shall not

be prohibited by the Congress prior to the Year one thousand eight hundred and eight, but a tax or duty may be imposed on such Importation, not exceeding ten dollars for each Person.

You often hear two schools of thought regarding the constitution. On one hand, many will say that this document is unflinching and must remain so to guarantee the freedoms and protections to each and every American citizen. On the other hand, others may say that this is a living document that is designed to and should change with the time, that it should evolve.

What do you think?

Should it remain firm or should it evolve?

Has it evolved enough or is there more work that must be done?

Is it possible that both arguments are merely the result of a well orchestrated distraction that prevents us all from seeing thing the way that they really are?

Domestically, slave trading continued and was pushed forward mostly by the need for labor in the developing cotton plantations. The plantations of the southeastern United States were flourishing and held large numbers slaves that were required for agricultural production. If you remember, one of the cultural requirements for mainstream slavery was surplus resources with cotton being that prominent resource in the south demanding labor to extract it. Forced migration further south resulted from less need to the north and more of a need for slave labor in the deeper south. No thought was given to splitting up families to make that happen. The slave population in the south was said to have reached 4 million by the time the practice was abolished.

Near the end of the practice of slavery (as most know it) in America, the west was being settled and developed and proponents of slavery were making the case that the practice should be expanded as more western territory was acquired. The reason for this, again, was money and power; power in the form of political power to maintain the balance of power between the north and the south. The north was in opposition to this which eventually led to the Civil War which, in turn, effectively ended what most people understand as slavery in the United States. The Confiscation Acts, the Emancipation Proclamation, and the Thirteenth Amendment to the United States Constitution served as the legal basis for the same.

President Abraham Lincoln issued the Emancipation Proclamation on January 1, 1863. At this time, the nation was approaching the third year of the bloody Civil War. The proclamation was written as follows;

By the President of the United States of America:

A Proclamation.

Whereas, on the twenty-second day of September, in the year of our Lord one thousand eight hundred and sixty-two, a proclamation was issued by the President of the United States, containing, among other things, the following, to wit:

"That on the first day of January, in the year of our Lord one thousand eight hundred and sixty-three, all persons held as slaves within any State or designated part of a State, the people whereof shall then be in rebellion against the United States, shall be then, thenceforward, and forever free; and the Executive Government of the United States, including the military and naval authority thereof, will recognize and maintain the freedom of such persons, and will do no act or acts to repress such persons, or any of them, in any efforts they may make for their actual freedom.

"That the Executive will, on the first day of January aforesaid, by proclamation, designate the States and parts of States, if any, in which the people thereof, respectively, shall then be in rebellion against the United States; and the fact that any State, or the people thereof, shall on that day be, in good faith, represented in the Congress of the United States by members chosen thereto at elections wherein a majority of the qualified voters of such State shall have participated, shall, in the absence of strong countervailing testimony, be deemed conclusive evidence that such State, and the people thereof, are not then in rebellion against the United States."

Now, therefore I, Abraham Lincoln, President of the United States, by virtue of the power in me vested as Commander-in-Chief, of the Army and Navy of the United

States in time of actual armed rebellion against the authority and government of the United States, and as a fit and necessary war measure for suppressing said rebellion, do, on this first day of January, in the year of our Lord one thousand eight hundred and sixty-three, and in accordance with my purpose so to do publicly proclaimed for the full period of one hundred days, from the day first above mentioned, order and designate as the States and parts of States wherein the people thereof respectively, are this day in rebellion against the United States, the following, to wit:

Arkansas, Texas, Louisiana, (except the Parishes of St. Bernard, Plaquemines, Jefferson, St. John, St. Charles, St. James Ascension, Assumption, Terrebonne, Lafourche, St. Mary, St. Martin, and Orleans, including the City of New Orleans) Mississippi, Alabama, Florida, Georgia, South Carolina, North Carolina, and Virginia, (except the forty-eight counties designated as West Virginia, and also the counties of Berkley, Accomac, Northampton, Elizabeth City, York, Princess Ann, and Norfolk, including the cities of Norfolk and Portsmouth[)], and which excepted parts, are for the present, left precisely as if this proclamation were not issued.

And by virtue of the power, and for the purpose aforesaid, I do order and declare that all persons held as slaves within said designated States, and parts of States, are, and henceforward shall be free; and that the Executive government of the United States, including the military and naval authorities thereof, will recognize and maintain the freedom of said persons.

And I hereby enjoin upon the people so declared to be free to abstain from all violence, unless in necessary self-defence; and I recommend to them that, in all cases when allowed, they labor faithfully for reasonable wages.

And I further declare and make known, that such persons of suitable condition, will be received into the armed service of the United States to garrison forts, positions, stations, and other places, and to man vessels of all sorts in said service.

And upon this act, sincerely believed to be an act of justice, warranted by the Constitution, upon military necessity, I invoke the considerate judgment of mankind, and the gracious favor of Almighty God.

In witness whereof, I have hereunto set my hand and caused the seal of the United States to be affixed.

Done at the City of Washington, this first day of January, in the year of our Lord one thousand eight hundred and sixty three, and of the Independence of the United States of America the eighty-seventh.

By the President: ABRAHAM LINCOLN

WILLIAM H. SEWARD, Secretary of State.

Of utmost importance is the fact that the Emancipation Proclamation did not set all slaves free. That was a fact that I was never taught about in school. It declared free only those slaves living in states not under Union control. William

Seward, Lincoln's secretary of state, commented, "We show our sympathy with slavery by emancipating slaves where we cannot reach them and holding them in bondage where we can set them free."

President Lincoln was fully aware of the irony, but he did not want to antagonize the slave states loyal to the Union by setting their slaves free.

Another fact regarding the "freeing" of the African slaves in America was that the Emancipation Proclamation, essentially, only gave them what could be considered residency in the United States and not citizenship. It wasn't until the 14th Amendment to the United States Constitution came about that these newly freed slaves were granted citizenship and the rights of that status.

The 14th Amendment reads as follows:

Amendment XIV

Section 1.

All persons born or naturalized in the United States, and subject to the jurisdiction thereof, are citizens of the United States and of the state wherein they reside. No state shall make or enforce any law which shall abridge the privileges or immunities of citizens of the United States; nor shall any state deprive any person of life, liberty, or property, without due process of law; nor deny to any person within its jurisdiction the equal protection of the laws.

Section 2.

Representatives shall be apportioned among the several states according to their respective numbers, counting the whole number of persons in each state, excluding Indians not taxed. But when the right to vote at any election for the choice of electors for President and Vice President of the United States, Representatives in Congress, the executive and judicial officers of a state, or the members of the legislature thereof, is denied to any of the male inhabitants of such state, being twenty-one years of age, and citizens of the United States, or in any way abridged, except for participation in rebellion, or other crime, the basis of representation therein shall be reduced in the proportion which the number of such male citizens shall bear to the whole number of male citizens twenty-one years of age in such state.

Section 3.

No person shall be a Senator or Representative in Congress, or elector of President and Vice President, or hold any office, civil or military, under the United States, or under any state, who, having previously taken an oath, as a member of Congress, or as an officer of the United States, or as a member of any state legislature, or as an executive or judicial officer of any state, to support the Constitution of the United States, shall have engaged in insurrection or rebellion against the same, or given aid or comfort to the enemies thereof. But Congress may, by a vote of two-thirds of each House, remove such disability.

Section 4.

The validity of the public debt of the United States, authorized by law, including debts incurred for payment of pensions and bounties for services in suppressing insurrection or rebellion, shall not be questioned. But neither the United States nor any state shall assume or pay any debt or obligation incurred in aid of insurrection or rebellion against the United States, or any claim for the loss or emancipation of any slave; but all such debts, obligations and claims shall be held illegal and void.

Section 5.

The Congress shall have power to enforce, by appropriate legislation, the provisions of this article.

Notice how when the three things that one could not be deprived of were stated...freedom was not one of them. The three things mentioned were life, liberty, and property. Of course, one could argue that liberty and freedom are essentially the same thing. The are not.

Freedom vs Liberty

The terms "freedom" and "liberty" are often tossed around without regard, especially by politicians. It is for this reason that their meanings are almost synonymous and used interchangeably. That's confusing – and can be dangerous – because their definitions are actually quite different.

"Freedom" is predominantly an internal construct. Holocaust survivor Viktor Frankl, who wrote Man's Search For Meaning, said it well: "Everything can be taken from a man but one thing: the last of the human freedoms – to choose one's attitude in any given set of circumstances, to choose one's own way (in how he approaches his circumstances)."

In other words, to be free is to take ownership of what goes on between your ears, to be autonomous in thoughts first and actions second. Your freedom to act a certain way can be taken away from you – but your attitude about your circumstances cannot – making one's freedom predominantly an internal construct. In layman's terms, freedom exists in the mind. It is your thinking that determines whether you are a slave or if you are free.

In contrast, "liberty" is predominantly an external construct. It's the state of being free within society from oppressive restrictions imposed by authority on one's way of life, behavior, or political views. The ancient Stoics knew this and so did the Founding Fathers of the United States. The Founding Fathers wisely noted the distinction between negative and positive liberties, and arranged them into specific codes in the U.S. Constitution and Bill of Rights. Ultimately, freedom is a God given right while liberty is granted by the state. As such, liberty can be withdrawn by the state while freedom must be surrendered by the individual.

Another important consideration is that of the meaning of "emancipation". One such meaning of emancipation is to *free from restraint, control, or the power of another especially...to free from bondage.* When the slaves were emancipated, they were freed from the restraint, control, and power of their slave masters. I submit to you that the restraint, control, and power that we are speaking of was not removed, dissolved or done away with. It was not eliminated but merely transformed. Perhaps, a better word to describe it would be "transferred". After all, that restraint, control, and power was simply transferred from the individual (slave master) to the state (United States Government).

Transforming Slavery

NOW YOU SEE IT...NOW YOU DON'T

Slavery 2.0

So what did slavery in America teach us?

It served as a recent reminder, a reenactment of sorts, of a phenomenon that has occurred over and over again in the past and will, most likely, repeat itself at some point in the future. What is peculiar about this last iteration is the way it was manipulated in such a way as to make it almost purely about race, as far as a qualifier goes. Equally as peculiar is the interesting way in which it has been related to the generations following it so as to muddy the waters in regards to the basic nature of it and the primary purpose of its use. As a mentioned before, race was used as construct upon which to create a focus of effort in creating and maintaining a slave labor force but it was money (in my humble opinion) that was the underlying influence that guided the major decisions regarding slavery.

Another lesson was that when slavery "ended", sharecropping took its place on the agricultural scene. This was an arrangement in which a tenant occupied a piece of land with the landowners permission provided the tenant remit a share of the crops produced to the landowner based on their established agreement. What we saw with this wasn't actually a cultural change that made slavery no longer acceptable or needed; instead, what we saw was a cultural change that made THAT FORM of slavery no longer acceptable or needed.

With the South having been devastated by war, the planters (plantation owners) had plenty of land but little "money" for wages or taxes. On the other hand, most of the "former slaves" had the ability to do work but no "money" and no land and they didn't want to do the kind of gang labor that was typical of "slavery". As you will realize by the end of this book, this was a more of a matter of perception than it was a matter of fact. One solution to this was the sharecropping system focused on cotton, which was the only crop that could generate cash for the croppers, landowners, merchants and the tax collector (cash crop).

It's important to note that poor white farmers (who had done little cotton farming the past) needed cash too and became sharecroppers. Why? Not because of race but because they needed the money.

This was also the point at which the prison system that we are familiar with today was first establish in the United States. The Thirteenth Amendment, ratified in 1865, made slavery and involuntary servitude unconstitutional in the United States "except as punishment for crime." When slavery ended in the south, a huge need for labor was created. The need was greater than one that sharecropping would be able to fill. The criminal justice system became one of the primary means of continuing the legalized involuntary servitude of African descendents.

At first, states passed discriminatory laws to arrest and imprison large numbers of black people. Next, they leased prisoners to private individuals and corporations in a system of convict leasing. This resulted in dangerous conditions, abuse, and death. So, while states profited, the prisoners earned no pay and faced inhumane and often deadly work conditions. Ultimately, thousands of black people were forced into a brutal system that historians have called "worse

FROM PLANTATIONS TO PRISONS

than slavery."

By the middle of the 20th century, most states had abandoned convict leasing because of industrialization and political pressure and extended slavery through chain gangs and prison farms. You can still see this legacy today as it influences the criminal justice system in places like Louisiana State Penitentiary. The Louisiana State Penitentiary was nicknamed "Angola" after the provenance of the enslaved people who worked the same land when it was a plantation. The prison requires its inmates to work in the fields. Eighty percent of Angola's imprisoned men are black, and one warden was quoted comparing the grounds to "a big plantation in days gone by."

In retrospect, the justification for slavery mere transformed from;

They deserve it because of who they are or what they believe

To

They deserve it because of what they have done or have failed to do.

Stay with me…

This gives rise to two major questions that we must answer before we can proceed;

What is Slavery?

And

What is Money?

Since we've spent this first portion of this book describing slavery and its influences at several different time periods, in various circumstances, and in different parts of the world, this question simply requires a bit of clarification.

Dictionary.com defines slavery as: *a person who is the property of and wholly subject to another; a bond servant. a person entirely under the domination of some influence or person.*

The word "influence" is extremely important here.

USLegal.com, in regards to slavery law and legal definition states: *A slave is a person owned by someone and slavery is the state of being under the control of someone where a person is forced to work for another. A slave is considered as a property of another as the one controlling them purchases them or owns them from their birth.*

The second definition appears to be more in line with the traditional thought process when one hears the words "slave" or "slavery". The reality of it is more likely best described by a merger of the two definitions.

Does it make sense to say that an "influence" can dominate a person from the time of their birth and, if that be the case, that phenomenon should fit the definition of slavery?

What bears further scrutiny is the use of terminology in this area, particularly in regards to the use of the term "slave" and the use of the term "indentured servant".

Harriet Tubman

HARRIET TUBMAN ESCAPED SLAVERY IN THE AMERICAN SOUTH

I had reasoned this out in my mind, there was one of two things I had a right to, liberty or death; if I could not have one, I would have the other.
- Harriet Tubman

Harriet Tubman was born Araminta Ross, her nickname was "Minty". She was both a political activist and an American abolitionist. Born as a slave, she escaped and was credited as making at least thirteen missions into slavery territory to rescue others from the perils of slavery in the south. She rescued mostly family and friends, approximately 70 people in total. She accomplished this by using what was known as the Underground Railroad. The Underground Railroad was a network of secret routes and safe houses that came into existence during the mid-1800s and used by slaves to escape into the free states. She also played a major role in the raid on Harpers Ferry. During the Civil War, she served as an armed scout and spy for the Union Army.

I grew up like a neglected weed - ignorant of liberty, having no experience of it.
- Harriet Tubman

Her parents, Harriet Green and Ben Ross were owned by Mary Pattison Brides. As was the case with many slaves, the exact year and place of her birth were unknown but it is pretty certain that she was born between 1815 and 1825. She claimed three different birth years in her Civil War widow's pensions records (1820, 1822, and 1825) indicating that she wasn't sure of her birth year. herself.

Harriet's mother was assigned to work in the "big house" and barely had any time for her own family. It was because of this that Harriet was charged with looking after her younger siblings. This was the norm in large families. As a testament to the brutality and backward thinking of her enslavement as a child, Harriet was hired out as a nursemaid and was ordered to watch over a baby as it slept; when the baby awoke and cried, Harriet was whipped as if it had been her fault. She even told of a day in which she was given five lashes with the whip before breakfast. Although she found ways to resist such as wearing extra layers of clothing and running away, she wore the scars of her childhood mistreatment for the rest of her life.

I never had anything good, no sweet, no sugar; and that sugar, right by me, did look so nice, and my mistress's back was turned to me while she was fighting with her husband, so I just put my fingers in the sugar bowl to take one lump, and maybe she heard me, for she turned and saw me. The next minute, she had the rawhide down.
- Harriet Tubman

While still a child, Harriet also worked at the home of a plantation owner named James Cook. Even after becoming sick with measles, she was made to check the muskrat traps in the nearby marshes. After becoming increasingly ill, Cook sent her back to Brodess and she was nursed back to health by her mother. Soon thereafter, Brodess hired her out again. As she grew older and stronger, she was assigned more strenuous duties like working in the forest, driving oxen, plowing and hauling logs.

As I lay so sick on my bed, from Christmas till March, I was always praying for poor ole master. 'Pears like I didn't do nothing but pray for ole master. 'Oh, Lord, convert ole master;' 'Oh, dear Lord, change dat man's heart, and make him a Christian.'
- Harriet Tubman

As a child who could not read, Harriet's mother told her Bible stories. Although the exact nature of her faith was not certain, she was known to have a passionate faith in God. After apparently having developed her own belief system, to an extent, she rejected the teachings of the New Testament that endorsed slavery and urged slaves to be obedient to their masters and found her direction in the Old Testament with its tales of deliverance. She was devout. She began experiencing dreams and visions interpreting them as God revealing truths to her.

She escaped from slavery in 1849 by running to Philadelphia. Almost immediately, she began returning to Maryland to rescue family members who remained enslaved by escorting small groups of them out of the state on group at a time. Over time, she led dozens of slaves out of bondage traveling using night as a cover and in secrecy. In 1950, the

Fugitive Slave Act was passed by the United States Congress. The Act required that all escaped slaves, upon capture, be returned to their masters forcing the cooperation of officials and citizens of the free states. This made it increasingly difficult to stay hidden in Philadelphia causing Harriet to help guide fugitive slaves farther north into the former territories of the British Empire in North America. She also helped fugitive slaves find work so that they could support themselves financially.

She worked for the Union Army once the Civil War began. First, she served as a cook and a nurse and later she became a scout and spy. Harriet Tubman was the first woman to lead an armed expedition in the war demonstrating that she was just as capable and suited as a man for the task. An accomplishment of note was that in guiding the raid at Combahee Ferry, she helped to liberate more than 700 slaves. She also fought on a different kind of battlefield, the battle for women's suffrage (the right to vote in elections) until she became ill passing away in 1913. After her death, she became a symbol of courage and freedom.

What can we learn from the story of Harriet Tubman?

We can learn that the human spirit can remain strong even under the most horrendous of circumstances.

We can learn that the desire for freedom is innate.

We can learn the importance and value of, after becoming free, reaching back and helping others find freedom.

We can learn just how much of an impact that one person can make no matter where they began and regardless of the circumstances of their birth…with a strong enough desire and a little help.

Consideration:

Harriet Tubman experience a harsh upbringing in which there was, seemingly, no regard for her as a human being. Having been born into slavery, she had never experienced life as a free person. She had, on the other hand, experienced caring for another human being as it was primarily her responsibility to care for her younger siblings. As their caretaker, she understood that survival depended on more than just love and affection. She was aware of many of the other requirements of having ones needs met. Even as a slave, she became aware of the power and necessity of having money.

One of the things that made her aware of this was the fact that her master was constantly hiring her out for work. She understood that it wasn't because he wanted to be benevolent or to help a friend. He was hurting for money. He was willing to do whatever it took, in a business sense, to create the cash flow that he so desperately needed which included hiring her out to someone who would pay regardless of her physical condition at the time. In his mind, she had to earn her keep. If not, she was useless to him.

She was also aware that part of being a whole human being was being able to provide for one's needs on one's own. It was for this reason that she was adamant about not only helping other slaves to escape but also about finding them useful employment after doing so. Understanding the value and power of money, Harriet understood that freedom meant more than just not being physically enslaved. She knew that they would never really be free until and unless they could sustain themselves financially.

A Slave by Any Other Name...

TWO SIDES OF THE SAME COIN

A name, in the most simple perspective is a term used for identification. In a lot of cases, that's where it ends. It simply is what it is. What is not simple is that terminology teaches us that the context in which a word is written or spoken can give the word specific meanings and these meanings can change depending on the context. The opposite is true as well. Different words can have the same meaning depending on the context in which they are used. Often, the deeper meaning of the word along with the connection of the different words becomes obscured. The result is that we no longer understand that two separate words indicate the same general condition. I say general because we have to look at it in a broader sense to really understand the impact. The details and specifics are what can throw us completely off the trail of the truth. When these terms are used to reference slavery, there are questions that must be asked.

Is indentured servitude essentially the same as slavery?

Is there really a significant enough difference between the two to warrant a separation, or at least the level of separation that we typically see, when referencing certain conditions?

How many times have you heard someone say something about a group of people not actually being slaves but rather they were indentured servants?

If you listen closely, statements such as this have the effect of revealing the true intent which is to minimize the seriousness of the state of indenture while simultaneously reducing the scope of the slave industry substantially. Pay close attention to the "difference" that is often stated as separating the two. It's usually either permission or compensation.

According to Investopedia,

Indentured servitude refers to a labor contract where someone is required to work for a landowner or another individual, typically for a period of five to seven years, in exchange for an expensive passage out of Europe.

That is but one definition and falls short of defining what indentured servitude really is.

Wikipedia provided a better definition in describing an indentured servants as follows:

An indentured servant or indentured laborer is an employee (indenturee) within a system of unfree labor who is bound by a signed or forced contract (indenture) to work for a particular employer for a fixed time. The contract often lets the employer sell the labor of an indenturee to a third party. Indenturees usually enter into an indenture for a specific payment or other benefit, or to meet a legal obligation, such as debt bondage. On completion of the contract, indentured servants were given their freedom, and occasionally plots of land. In many countries, systems of indentured labor have now been outlawed, and are banned by the Universal Declaration of Human Rights as a form of slavery.

This, more lengthy, definitions needs to be pulled apart to clarify your understanding.

Let's start with "unfree" labor. Unfree labor refers to work relationships, especially those from the 16th century forward, in which people are employed against their will with the threat of;

Destitution - or poverty pertains to the scarcity or lack of a significant amount of material possessions or money. Destitution, specifically, refers to the complete lack of the means necessary to meet one's or one's families basic personal needs like food, clothing, and shelter.

Detention - Detention is the lawful holding of a person by removing his or her freedom or liberty at that time. What this basically amounts to is depriving them of their liberty to come and go as they please. The term can also be used when referring to property.

Violence - The World Health organization defines violence as "the intentional use of physical force or power, threatened or actual, against oneself, another person, or against a group or community, which either results in or has a high likelihood of resulting in injury, death, psychological harm, maldevelopment, or deprivation." Power being the capacity of an individual to influence the conduct (behavior) of others.

Compulsion - this one is very interesting, see the following three definitions;

1. An irrational need or irresistible urge to perform some action, often despite negative consequences.
2. The use of authority, influence, or other power to force (compel) a person or persons to act.
3. The lawful use of violence (i.e. by the administration).

An indentured servitude relationship could also be caused by the threat (actual or imagined) of other forms of extreme hardship to themselves or members of their families.

When you think about it, doesn't that really cover just about every work relationship that exists?

Let me explain…

Each and every hour of labor generated in mainstream America has the fear of one of the preceding outcomes motivating the laborer to act.

The term "indenture" just means that a contract has been established that reflects an agreement to cover a debt or a purchase obligation. So, with that in mind, one can reasonable conclude that rather than slavery and indentured servitude being two different things, indentured servitude is merely a modification of slavery in which "additional" conditions have been added (i.e. treatment, compensation, etc.). In any case, the fear of destitution, detention, violence, or compulsion motivates the laborer to act in that capacity with the primary difference being which of those four threats is the greatest in that particular situation. When thinking of slavery, one most likely thinks of violence. When termed as indentured servitude, one likely thinks more about destitution.

So, once again, our focus must turn towards money. In this instance, and more specifically, we are talking about debt.

Debt can be defined as that state when something (usually money) is owed by one party who is called the debtor or borrower to another party who is called the creditor or lender. It can be further defined as a deferred payment, or series of payments, that is owed in the future. Of real importance is the fact that the term doesn't always refer to economic value (but usually does) and can be used metaphorically to refer to moral obligations and other interactions not based on economic value. This is the root of the concept that a person can owe a "debt" of gratitude when someone has helped them in some way. Of equal importance is the fact that even though the immediate debt may not be of "economic value" you can be certain that the the payment of that debt, at some point, translate into an act or transfer of ownership that does. Therefore, economic value usually exists just maybe not in the primary position but, instead, may be identified in the secondary or tertiary position.

This debt can then become the basis for enslavement which then creates a situation which can be called debt bondage, debt slavery, or bonded labor.

One definition of the term *bondage* is: *the state of being a slave.*

Now it becomes clear as day that indentured servitude, being based on the fact that some debt exists, is merely slavery by a different name. A slave by any other name…is still a slave.

Additional facts that should be remembered and help to drive that point home are:

- Often the terms of repayment are not clearly or reasonable stated.
- The person holding the debt doesn't intend to ever admit the debt has been repaid.
- The services required to pay the debt may be undefined.
- The services duration may be undefined
- Undefined service terms may lead to a demand for indefinite service.
- Debt bondage can be passed from generation to generation.

To further illustrate the fact that debt bondage (indentured servitude) is really a form of slavery, one simply has to look at the decision that was arrived at by the United Nations that classified it as modern day slavery. That being said, there is no universally agreed upon definition of modern slavery. In addition, those in slavery are often difficult to identify. On top of that, adequate statistics are often not available. So here's the big question, "Why is it so difficult to identify those in slavery?"

Why is it so hard to tell a person who is a slave from a person who is not?

Shouldn't this be like super easy?

Think about it!

The reason is because the activities are exactly the same in many cases.

That should make you think…real hard.

Consider this, in many countries, the systems of indentured servitude have been outlawed or banned by the Universal Declaration of Human Rights as a form of slavery. The Universal Declaration of Human Rights was adopted by the United Nations in 1948 and is comprised of 30 articles that serve to affirm an individuals rights.

Hang in there, and keep all of this in mind because I'm going somewhere with this.

Now that we have established what slavery is and the fact that it comes in various forms, let's take a look at what creates the perceived separation of slavery or "unfree labor" from non-slavery or "free-labor". In order for us to do that, we have to clarify at least two things; the first is the nature of freedom and the second is the nature of compensation.

Freedom

What is freedom…really? The definition of freedom would vary a great deal depending on who you ask. A common answer would be that freedom is merely the state of being free or at liberty rather than being in confinement or under physical restraint. For others, the definition would go far beyond that of a physical nature. To some it means independence. Have you ever given thought to what freedom really means to you? Let's dig into the concept of freedom a little bit deeper and see what we find.

Let's have a good look at three different definitions of freedom;

Freedom Definition 1 - *The power or right to act, speak, or think a one wants without hindrance or restraint.*

Firstly, powers and rights are two entirely different things although used in a way that makes them appear to be strong synonyms in this definition. While power alludes to the ability to do a thing, rights allude to the legal entitlement to do a thing. Although one has the entitlement to do a thing, the power to do so can be modifies by the latter portion of the definition wherein it states *without hindrance or restraint.* This is were it becomes tricky. Hindrance can be thought of as anything that provides resistance, delay, or obstruction to something or someone. At first glance, one might read these words and immediately come in to the frame of mind that a hindrance must be some type of physical obstruction but that is very far from being the case. That hindrance can be self imposed in the form of "restraint" which is defined as *a measure or condition that keeps someone or something under control or within limits.* So, what would be the source of this? Again, at first glance, the source would appear to be the individual themselves but in actuality it would be a response to an outside stimuli. This person who is lacking freedom under this first definition is this state due to fear of an eventual outcome based on an outside influence.

Remember when we discussed destitution, detention, violence and compulsion? How often can one truly express themselves (especially on sensitive topics or legal matters) without some legitimate fear of reprisal? I submit to you that the impingement of that individuals freedom is rarely done at the time that the words are spoken but rather in some form of retribution at a latter time. And that form of retribution typically falls under one of the four aforementioned ways of getting someone to provide "unfree labor" or act against their will except in this case it is responsible for inaction rather than action. One can be enslaved and being urged to perform and one can also be enslaved and urged not to perform.

Freedom Definition 2 - Absence of subjection to foreign domination or despotic government.

There are a couple of things here that should be pointed out and addressed. Firstly, Subjection occurs when a person, group, or government forces another person (or group of people) to submit or be controlled. In Freedom Definition 2, there are two modifiers placed behind that word; the first being that of foreign domination and the second being a "despotic" government. What is meant by "despotic"? This is a form of government in which a single entity rules with absolute power. Normally, that entity is an individual, the despot, as in an autocracy where we have a king with real powers. It can also refer to societies which limit respect and power to specific groups within the population.

Now, here is the million dollar question! Does it really matter whether or not that power is being welded by a single person or a group of people, or if that power is foreign or domestic, if the effect of the welding of such power is the same? For instance, if one were to get their ass kicked, does it really matter if it was one person or a group of people that did it or if the one (s) who did it are American or not when it comes down to whether or not one has just gotten his ass kicked? An ass kicking is an ass kicking, plain and simple.

Freedom Definition 3 - The state of not being imprisoned or enslaved.

This third definition is the one that is seemingly the most simple and straightforward. In terms of imprisonment, that is easy enough to follow as in not physically incarcerated. The second part, however, is not so easily explained away. As was discussed earlier, enslavement is not as cut and dry as one would initially think in that enslavement can come in many forms. One of these forms is to be in a state in which one has lost their freedom of choice or action.

So, we've been given three different definitions of freedom, none of which; clearly distinguish between true freedom and being under the influence of some outside influence or power. This is especially true in the case that the outside influence has disrupted the internal decision making process to the extent that it becomes difficult to distinguish whether that influence or the the individual making the decision is actually at blame for any semblance of the loss of freedom.

Let me clarify...

One can safely say that, based on all of the definitions of freedom we have been given, that whether or not one is free or not all comes down to one thing; choice. It comes down to whether or not the individual in question has the ability to choose.

Right?

Okay then, now that we've gotten to this point, there is another important question that we must ask if we are to gain a better understanding of what freedom really is and that is this, "What is choice?"

We keep hearing that buzz word whenever there is a debate or discussion about free will; which is the lynchpin in a discussion about whether or not some type of force has been applied and subsequently whether the actor is acting in the capacity of a slave or not.

So let's get to it.

Choice

What does choice mean for you?

I used to think of choice in the most simplest of terms. I figured that it was the ability to select between a set of given options. As I moved forward in my journey to freedom, the way that I viewed choice began to change. I began to think of choice as not only the ability to choose between a set of given option but also the ability to develop new options on my own. To blaze my own trail by creating a path that had not existed before. I saw it as having the latitude to design my own life instead of picking a variance of one that had been chosen for me. There were times that I felt that I had no choices, no options. At some point, I realized that if I was ever to become free I had to learn to think outside of the box.

Ultimately, choice is the selection of one option or a set of options from amongst two or more options or sets of options.

So, let's clarify what it is so that there can be no doubt as to whether or not it exists I a given situation.

The process of choosing includes the following:

Judging - forming an opinion or conclusion about.

Options - things that are or may be chosen.

Selecting - carefully choosing as being the best or the most suitable.

So, we can see that in order for choice to exist we must have options about which to form opinions or conclusions and then have the ability to select one of those options.

Can you think of ANY situation in which there are not at least two options (no matter how undesirable) about which to form opinions or conclusions that one then has the ability to select one of those options?

If you can think of ANY situation like this, please send an email to Admin@ShermanRivers.com with a brief explanation of the situation. Why? Because I would really love to know about it! I can't think of one single solitary situation in the past, present, or future in which choice does not exist.

Not one.

What does this mean?

It means that slavery itself, yes, being enslaved by another man or woman and forced to labor for his or her benefit...is a choice.

Sounds crazy doesn't it?

I should probably be very careful in saying that. I remember when Kanye West was verbally assaulted for saying the same thing but, hey, it is what it is!

It'd probably be easier to see where I'm coming from if we consider three complex motivators that can influence (there's that word again) the arrival at a choice. Let's take a look at them:

Cognition - Cognition is the mental action or process of acquiring knowledge and understanding through thought, experience, and the senses. Experience, in this case, can include negative outcomes that were produced as a result of a choice that was based on the power or right to take a specific action which inhibits one from making a similar choice at some point in the future. Cognitive processes use existing knowledge and generate new knowledge. Existing knowledge can be a source of fear, therefore, during the knowledge generating process, one can become enslaved through fear of a negative outcome (experience) and a desire to avoid it. That desire is a very powerful one. What are some negative outcomes that you have an intense desire to avoid?

Instinct - In living organisms, instinct is the inborn and natural tendency or urge towards a particular behavior which may be considered complex or consisting of many different and connected parts. One qualifier in determining whether a behavior is instinctive or not is whether the behavior is performed without being based on prior experience. In other words, unlike a behavior developed through the cognitive process, an instinctive behavior is not learned.

Feeling - In this instance, feeling is referring to the conscious quality of awareness or being aware of something externally rather than simple touch. Feeling can often be complicated to explain but for the purposes of this writing it is simplified in meaning to that which influences, informs, and biases people's judgments about truth or reality; it is the collection of the perceptions, experiences, expectations, personal or cultural understanding, and beliefs specific to a person. What are some things that you have very strong feelings about?

So, with those motivators driving the decision making process through the three basic steps of which it is composed, we can be sure of two things; the first thing that we can be sure of is that choice always exists. This is contrasted by the second thing that we can be sure of which is that the motivating factors within the decision making process can be so strong that the illusion is created that choice does not exist. This is exactly what it is, an illusion.

Choice

There is ALWAYS a choice to be made.

Can you recall a situation or circumstance in which you felt that you didn't have a choice?

Again, if you can think of ANY situation in which there are not at least two options (no matter how undesirable) about which to form opinions or conclusions that one then has the ability to select from...please let me know.

Compensation

As mentioned earlier, the second thing that creates the perceived separation of slavery or "unfree labor" from non-slavery or "free-labor" is the nature of compensation. In this instance, the type of compensation to which we are referring is that of financial compensation. As you may have picked up on by now, when moving into a new area or topic, I like to start off with the definition. This way we can be sure that we are having a conversation about the same thing and that everyone involved has a clear understanding of what the terms that we use in dialogue really mean. Financial compensation refers to the act of providing a person (legal person) with money or other things of economic value in exchange for their goods, labor, or to provide for the costs of injuries that they have incurred. "Money", there is that word again!

Let's have a good look at the various types of compensation.

Damages

Under the body of law derived from past judicial decisions of courts and similar tribunals, damages are a monetary fix as compensation for loss or injury. If an entity claiming damages can show that a breach of duty has caused a foreseeable loss. Typically, damages are paid when there is damage to property or mental/physical injury. Various subcategories of damages exist to address compensatory damages. Important to recognize is the fact that, although damages are categorized and layered in what seems like a trillion different ways, one fact remains, All damages seem to have a monetary equivalent. Somehow, some way, it all comes back to money.

Nationalization

Nationalization is a series of actions or steps taken in order to transform private assets into public assets by bringing them under the possession of a national government or state or some other public body. Nationalization can actually occur without any compensation being paid! All a government truly needs is a good reason (or excuse) to seize property and claim ownership. The means by which the former owners gained possession of the property in the first place is usually reason enough to take that action.

Payment

Payment is the bargaining of a measure of benefit for one entity to another in exchange for goods, services, or to settle a legal matter. Payment can take many forms including; barter, ownership, and debt but, in most cases, it takes the form of money. There's that word again! Here is an interesting fact; the laws normally require someone to accept the country's currency (legal tender) up to a certain point. What this means is that if someone owed you something specific but instead wanted to pay you in the country's currency in which you reside, you would have to accept that as payment.

More on money and currency later.

Another huge consideration in payment is the number of parties involved in a transaction. For example, a bank wire transfer would involve 4 parties; the purchaser, the seller, the sending bank, and the receiving bank. A cash transaction would require three parties at a minimum; the seller, the purchaser, and the issuer of the currency. Only two parties would be required in a barter transaction, those parties being the purchaser and the seller. The less parties involved, the less interference and control outside of the purchaser and the seller.

Remuneration

The pay or other compensation that is provided in exchange for an employee's services are called remuneration. Some examples of remuneration include:

Commission - a form of variable pay for services rendered or products sold. Payments are often calculated using a percentage of revenue earned.

Compensation

Executive Compensation - financial and non-financial compensation and other non-financial rewards received by an executive from their firm for service to the organization. Usually, executive compensation is a mixture of salary, bonuses, benefits, shares of company stock.

Deferred Compensation - this is an arrangement in which a portion of an employee's income is paid out at a later date. You would find this with pension plans, retirement plans, and employee stock options. The main benefit of an arrangement such as this is the deferral of the taxes paid on those earnings until the time at which the employee receives the income. The downfall is that there is no way of knowing what the tax rate will be at that time.

Royalties - A royalty is a payment made by a licensee or franchisee to an owner of a particular asset for the right to ongoing use of that asset. Usually, the royalty is a percentage of the gross or net revenues resulting from the use of the asset. Royalties are put in place through the use of licensing agreements which define the terms under which an asset or resource may be used.

Salary - As a result of a contract used in labor law to attribute rights and responsibilities between parties to a bargain (employment contract), one form of payment that can be used is a salary. A salary is a fixed amount of money or compensation paid to an employee by an employer in return for work performed on a periodic basis and commonly paid in fixed intervals. In my experience, salaried employees tend to believe that they are more loyal and in some cases, more noble.

Wage -   As with a salary, a wage is monetary compensation paid to an employee for work performed. In contrast to the salary form of pay, wages are a fixed amount paid for each task completed, or at an hourly or daily rate, or based on an easily measured quantity of work done. Another interesting fact about wages is that wages are the foundation of the federal system of taxation in the United States of America. Woe unto the wage earner, for he wears a target on his back.

Employee Benefits - various types of non-wage compensation provided to employees in addition to their wages or salaries are called employee benefits. A laundry list of items fall into this category which include (but are not limited to) health insurance, dental insurance, sick leave, vacation time, profit sharing, daycare, housing, and more. In most cases, all of the aforementioned benefits are taxable to some extent. Retention is the reason for offering employee benefits. The theory is that more an employee feels economically secure, the more likely they are to stay with that employer.

Workers' Compensation - in the case of an employee that has been injured on the job, a form of insurance that can provide for the replacement of wages and also medical benefits is called workers' compensation. By spreading the liability of an employee injury throughout a collective, it could be assured that a single employer would not become insolvent under the weight of damages award to an injured employee.

Based on these forms of compensation, we can conclude that even though the definition of remuneration specifically refers to pay or "other compensation" that is provided in exchange for an employee's services, it is easier to view remuneration as money or the promise of money in certain situations given in exchange for an employee's services. We can say it's about many other things and offer a million different words, phrases, and definitions but the bottom line is that it al, everything, comes down to money. By law, everything has a monetary equivalent.

Allow me to quote an earlier passage from this writing,

> *Let's start with "unfree" labor. Unfree labor refers to work relationships, especially those from the 16th century forward, in which people are employed against their will with the threat of;*

> *Destitution - or poverty pertains to the scarcity or lack of a significant amount of material possessions or money. Destitution, specifically, refers to the complete lack of the means necessary to meet one's or one's families basic personal needs like food, clothing, and shelter.*

As we see, one of the threats that constitutes labor under slavery or indentured servitude is the threat of destitution. Material possessions and, "means" such as food, clothing, and shelter all translate into or have a monetary equivalent. Can you function in this society without money? Better yet, what are your choices regarding whether you even want to be a member of this society or not?

Next, we'll make sure that we are all on the same page regarding money and what that really is so that we can pick up the pace and paint a clear picture for you.

It's all about the money.

Note: A hint regarding the importance of money can be seen in the fact that at the time of this writing there have been at least 5 films and 2 television shows titled "Money".

I truly believe that statement. Slavery, in its various forms really is all about the money. Sure enough, there are conditions that prevail (in most instances) that give the false impression that the presiding reasons for slavery are motivated by something else. Race is one such thing. But what is race other than a construct that serves to create a separation among members of the same species. Recognizing this is important for one main reason; most people need to feel that the slave is different from them in some manner, less than them. Their belief system must be modified to this end to increase their comfort level with the idea of slavery, In the end though, even with other factors contributing, it really is about the money.

Money

Money can be defined as anything or verifiable record that is generally accepted as trade of value for tangible items and activities provided by other people and also the repayment of something owed. Taxes are a good example of something that is or can be owed.

Before we move forward, an important point should be made here.

Taxes are compulsory financial charges imposed upon a taxpayer by a governmental organization in order to pay for certain things that have been deemed necessary for the public good. Furthermore, if one fails to pay such taxes, or "resists", or "evades", it is punishable by law. Furthermore, taxes are considered either direct (income taxes) or indirect (sales tax) and may be paid in money or labor as its equivalent.

The first word that should jump out at you is the word "compulsory"

Compulsory: required by law or a rule; obligatory and/or involving or exercising compulsion; coercive.

Now, if you will, please allow your mind to travel back to the four threats that were listed and defined as having been the determining facts as to whether labor was free or not and thusly whether that labor was indentured servitude (slavery) or not. The last of these was compulsion which was defined as;

1. An irrational need or irresistible urge to perform some action, often despite negative consequences.
2. The use of authority, influence, or other power to force (compel) a person or persons to act.
3. The lawful use of violence (i.e. by the administration).

So we can conclude that taxes equate to the use of authority, influence, or government power to force a person or persons to pay money under the threat of the lawful use of violence. Looking further, the words "resist" and "evade" imply intent, an almost deviant intent, but what if someone simply "fails"?

For example, they simply do not do it.

Simple answer…it is punishable by law.

So, if we can move past the images and the history surrounding your perception of what slavery is, analyze the concept of slavery and the various definitions of the conditions that it is comprised of, and look at it in its most basic form we can see that the following two things are a matter of fact;

1 - Taxation, in that it is compulsory, is in and of itself a form of slavery

And

2 - Failure to pay taxes, in that it is punishable by law, in that legal punishment involves a conviction, leads to legal slavery as openly stated in the 13th amendment of the United States Constitution.

How's that for damned if you do and damned if you don't?

So, taxation is the legal and forceful extraction of... here comes that word again...money.

Back to the money...

Currency

Any form of money when in use or circulation as a medium of exchange is considered currency. Currencies are defined by governments and each type of currency has limited boundaries of acceptance. Currency can be classified into to monetary systems; commodity money and fiat money.

Commodity Money

Money, in emerging markets is usually established in a form whose value comes from a commodity of which it is made (commodity money). A commodity is a raw material or primary agricultural product that can be bought and sold, such as copper or coffee. When used as money the have value beyond that of a trading mechanism or a store of value.

Fiat Money

In modern monetary systems, the most common form of money is what is known as "fiat money". Fiat money is money that has no value as a physical commodity. Use value refers to the tangible features of a commodity which can satisfy some human requirement, want or need, or which serves a useful purpose. Instead of gaining its value from its intrinsic value, fiat money derives its value from being declared to be legal tender by a government. Legal tender is a medium of payment recognized by a legal system to be valid for meeting a financial obligation. Declaration as legal tender means that it must be accepted as a form of payment within the boundaries of the country, for"all debts, public and private".

Money Supply

The money supply is the total value of all of the monetary assets available in an area of the production, distribution, or trade, and consumption of goods and services by different agents at a specific time. These agents can be individuals, businesses, organizations, or governments. This data is typically recorded by the government or central bank of the country.

With a basic understanding of what money is, we can zoom in a little further on the United States of America by focusing on the currency in use in this country, the United States Dollar (USD).

What is a dollar?

First off, the United States isn't the only country that calls its currency "dollars". More than 20 countries refer to their currency as dollars. These countries include; Australia, Canada, Hong Kong, Jamaica, Liberia, Namibia, New Zealand, Singapore, Taiwan, and the United States. In addition to that, the U.S. dollar is also the official currency of the Caribbean Netherlands, East Timor, Ecuador, El Salvador, the Federated States of Micronesia, the Marshall Islands, Palau, and Zimbabwe.

Normally, one dollar is divided into 100 cents.

The U.S. dollar has nearly a century and a half long history since the delegates from 13 British colonies authorized the issue of early american currency in 1775. In 1792, these delegates created the United States dollar as the united States of America's standard unit of money. The term "dollar", itself, was already familiar to the masses having had been used since the time of European colonization beginning in the 6th century when it referred to the Spanish dollar. The Spanish dollar was used throughout territories of the Spanish empire and also known as the eight-real coin. This (piece of eight) was a silver coin of approximately 38mm in diameter and worth eight Spanish reales (unit of currency in Spain at the time). It was minted in the Spanish empire during the time following a monetary reform in 1497.

When the war between Great Britain and the thirteen colonies began in 1775, the Continental Congress started issuing Continental currency, paper money called Continentals. This currency was in denominations of dollars ranging from one sixth of a dollar to 80 dollars. A total of $241,552,780 in Continental currency was issued during the revolution. Within 5 years of the start of the revolution, the continental currency had lost so much value that it was only worth about one fortieth of its face value. Attempts to reform the currency were met with little success and by 1781 the currency had become worthless and stopped circulating.

In 1782, the idea for the creation of the first financial institution chartered by the United States was put forth culminating with the issuance of the U.S. dollar as a new currency in 1785. Along with that, came concerns about uncontrolled inflation and a similar collapse as the one that had occurred with the Continental currency. As a result, the gold and silver clause (contract clause) was included. This contract clause appears in the United States Constitution, Article I, section 10, clause 1. It prohibits a State from passing any law that "impairs the obligation of contracts" or "makes any thing but gold and silver coin a tender in payment of debts". The clause states the following;

No State shall enter into any Treaty, Alliance, or Confederation; grant Letters of Marque and Reprisal; coin Money; emit Bills of Credit; make any Thing but gold and silver Coin a Tender in Payment of Debts; pass any Bill of Attainder, ex post facto Law, or Law impairing the Obligation of Contracts, or grant any Title of Nobility.

The primary task of producing and circulating coinage was taken up by a newly created United States mint under the Coinage Act of 1792. The Act installed the U.S. dollar as the United States standard unit of money, established the U.S. Mint, and regulated the coinage of the United States. The mint was originally under the auspice of the Department of State until becoming a part of the Department of the Treasury with the Coinage Act of 1873.

In 1900, the United States passed the Gold Standard Act which stated:

...the dollar consisting of twenty-five and eight-tenths grains of gold nine-tenths fine, as established by section

thirty-five hundred and eleven of the Revised Statutes of the United States, shall be the standard unit of value, and all forms of money issued or coined by the United States shall be maintained at a parity of value with this standard...

Neutrality in war was the key to the United States maintaining its gold standard. It was the only country to do so without restrictions on imports or exports of gold from 1915 to 1917.

You may be wondering why the history lesson in regards to money or currency. Why is it so important to understand how money works? We've already seen that money is the driving factor behind the slavery mechanism in every form that it takes. If we don't understand the nature of money and how it works, we become and remain enslaved within a system and under a master who we don't understand.

The value of the American dollar was eventually unlinked from the value of gold during the early 1960's. President Nixon issued Executive order 11615 which ended the direct convertibility of dollars to gold. This was referred to as the Nixon Shock; a series of economic measures undertaken by Nixon in response to increasing inflation which included; wage freezes, price freezes, surcharges on imports, and the unilateral cancellation of the direct international convertibility of the Unites States dollar to gold. This marked the transition from the gold standard to a currency without intrinsic value through government regulation.

One of the driving forces behind all of this was uncontrolled inflation.

What is inflation and how does it work?

To put it bluntly, inflation is the nemesis of growth in terms of your money. It is the continued increase in the hypothetical daily measure of overall prices of goods and services in an economy over time. Likewise, inflation reflects a decrease in purchasing power per unit of money equaling a loss of real value. The opposite of inflation is deflation.

The most important point to knowing this is understanding the premise behind the controls that are put in place to regulate the flow of money. Much of this is done by the central banks. The central banks are the institutions that manage the currency, money supply, and interest rates of a state or two or more states that share the same currency and oversees their commercial banking system. The central bank has a monopoly on the total amount of any notes and coins circulating in the economy. In most developed nations, the central banks are institutionally independent from political interference.

This opens the door for another huge question.

Who controls the money?

Is it the government?

Is it some private entity?

If money is the primary factor regarding slavery, who are the real masters?

Maybe we could get closer to the answer to that question if we took a good look at taxation.

Taxes

A TAX FOR JUST ABOUT EVERYTHING

Taxation comes in many different forms and varieties and at all levels of government. Most notably at the federal level. I can see the logic behind them. A system of government would grind to a halt without them. But, does there need to be so many? When you really stop to think about the level of taxation in the United States, it almost becomes laughable. Some folks would argue that this is nothing compared to other places in the world but does that negate the point? I've learned to be wary of people who tend to justify an "evil" by bringing up a worse one. I've joked about it in the past by saying thats like someone getting beaten with a wooden baseball bat and expressing discontent and then someone responds by saying that in some places attackers use metal ones. I guess that makes it okay?

Some taxes are based on a percentage of an individual or households annual income while others are based on a flat rate percentage. Some of the forms in which these taxes are manifested are as wealth taxes, property taxes, sales taxes, value-added taxes, and payroll taxes, just to name a few.

Wealth Taxes

A levy on the total value of personal assets, including; bank deposits, real estate, assets in insurance and pension plans, ownership of unincorporated businesses, financial securities, and personal trusts. In most cases, an individual can deduct liabilities from the total amount.

Property Taxes

A tax whose amount is based on the value of a transaction or of property and is usually levied on real estate by the governing authority of the jurisdiction in which the property is located whether that be a national government, a federated state, a county or geographical region, or a municipality. In some cases, property taxes can even be levied by multiple jurisdictions against the same property.

Sales Taxes

A tax paid to a governing body for the sales of certain goods and services. These taxes are often collected at the point of sale by the seller and then remitted to the government by them. In cases where it is paid directly to the government by the purchaser, it is called a use tax. Certain goods and services may be excluded depending on the laws governing the transactions.

Value-Added Taxes

A type of tax based on the increase of value a product or service gains at each stage of production or distribution. It is usually a flat tax collected by the end retailer similar to a sales tax in nature. Usually implemented as a destination-based tax, it would be calculated based on the location of the consumer and applied to the sales price of the particular good or service.

Payroll Taxes

A tax imposed on employers or employees and usually calculated as a percentage of the salaries that employers pay their staff. Payroll taxes are usually split into two categories; one being deductions from an employee's wages, and the other being those paid by the employer based on the wages that they pay to the employee.

In theory, the purpose of taxes levied by the government is to raise revenue to fund the process of governing in itself or to alter prices in order to affect demand. Another important purpose is to service debt accumulated by the government during times when expenditures exceeded tax revenue.

Let's take a closer look at the latter reason - to service debt incurred by the government.

Here's a question, if a government can incur debt just like an individual can, can a government be subject to enslavement through debt just like an individual can be?

The Haitian Example

HAITI PAID A HEAVY PRICE FOR "FREEDOM"

The Spanish began to enslave the natives of the island of Hispaniola in 1492, shortly after Christopher Columbus sighted the island. The population of people living there when the Spanish arrived were forced to mine for gold and the island suffered under horrible working conditions and diseases brought there by the Europeans. Before long, the native population died out under these conditions and was replaced by slaves imported from Africa. Following the depletion of the gold mines, the Spanish colonizers were replaced by the French who set up a system of plantations.

Between the years of 1697 and 1804, over 800,00 West African slaves were imported into the Haitian island and their labor made Haiti one of the richest European colonies in the west. The plantations of the island produced sixty percent of France and Britain's coffee and three quarters of the world's sugar. Importation of slaves to that island accounted for one third of the entire African slave trade. The treatment of slaves there was also known to be some of the most cruel. Of a population totaling around 520,000 people in 1790, 425,00 were slaves.

The country of Haiti declared independence from France in 1804 after a series of conflicts beginning in 1791 and up until that time. These conflicts were between Haitian slaves, colonists, the armies of the British and French colonizers, and a number of other parties. After winning independence from France, Haiti became the first country, at least in the western hemisphere to be founded by former slaves. In order for France to recognize this independence, France (with the complicity of its allies) demanded that Haiti pay the French government and French slaveholders what would be equal to $21 billion dollars for the "theft" of the slaves own lives and for the land that they had turned into profitable sugar and coffee-producing plantations. The debt was financed by French banks (who never actually lent any money) and an American bank, Citibank. It was paid off in 1947.

So, here we see a situation in which an entire country was placed into a sort of debt bondage due to the requirement to repay a debt. A debt, mind you, that was placed on that country as a result of one basic desire - a desire for freedom from slavery. Making it worse, this was condoned by the international community. The debt was not repaid until 1947. Haiti raised funds through other debt to accomplish this and those loans carried interest. If the amount of the loan would have been invested, it would have grown to 69 trillion dollars by 2014 at a nominal rate of return at 4% after inflation. At an 8% annual return, that figure would have been 90 trillion dollars.

Ever heard the saying that crap rolls downhill? If you pay attention, its not long before you can clearly see a pattern developing in which the need to repay money to lenders causes governments to place the burden on the people who place a burden on other people and so on and so on. The individual usually ends up at the bottom of the hill standing in a puddle of liquified oozing foul smelling crap. It is a big puddle too, not one you could just take a step to the side and extricate yourself from. It is a global system. It is a system from which there is no escape.

Bringing it Together

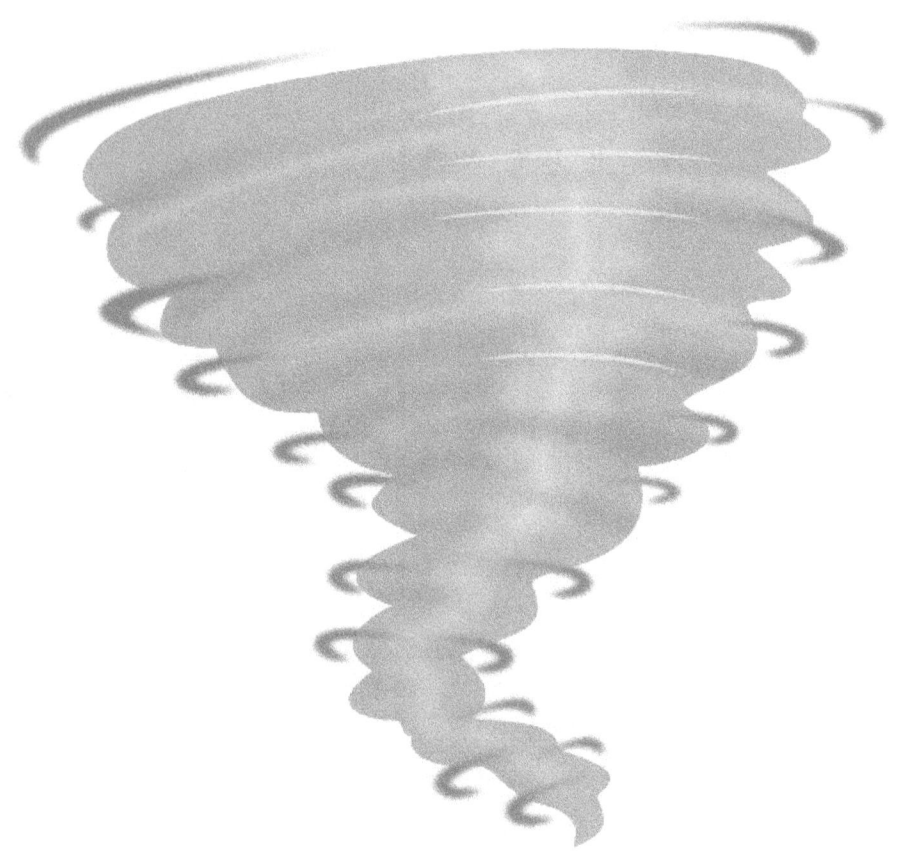

FREEDOM - DEFINING THE CONDITION

Now that we've taken the time to carefully look at slavery and money, we can see how the two marry up with one another to create an unpopular condition. So unpopular that anyone who has come close to addressing it usually attempts to disguise the true nature of the relationship by layering words and toying with definitions. For the financial machine to function, it must be constantly supplied with inputs of labor. It must be organized with a firm system of control. It all amounts to the restriction of freedom. Let's review the three definitions of freedom as they pertain to or are influenced by money.

Freedom Definition 1 - *The power or right to act, speak, or think a one wants without hindrance or restraint.*

Sounds great, doesn't it. That is until we are reminded of the fact that when we are in the employ of another, often, that freedom no longer exists. Technically, the First Amendment protects citizens from Congress enacting a law that would restrict an individual's right to say or express themselves "freely". That has since been expanded to include many actions by state and federal government. But, here's the catch, it only protects you from government actions. The government isn't the one paying you money as an employee if you are employed in the private sector. What can and can't be done in response to your exercising your rights varies based on who your employer is. For instance, a police officer can't arrest you because you wore a hat supporting a particular political candidate. But your boss could fire you for the very same reason. That doesn't sound like freedom. What do you think? How's that for hindrance or restraint?

Freedom Definition 2 - Absence of subjection to foreign domination or despotic government.

As I asked earlier in this book, does it really matter whether or not that power is being welded by a single person or a group of people, or if that power is foreign or domestic, if the effect of the welding of such power is the same? For example, if that power is being used to extract money from its citizens in the form of taxation, does it matter who's doing it? Many people reading it might say, yes. And I would say that it is a conditioned response. They have been conditioned to respond that way lest they suffer the pains that accompany the feeling of disloyalty to their country or a lack of patriotism. If one doesn't agree with what their government does or how it conducts business, that one must be anti-government or against their country, right?

Freedom Definition 3 - The state of not being imprisoned or enslaved.

As I mentioned earlier, this third definition is the one that is seemingly the most simple and straightforward. The first part meaning not physically incarcerated. The second part, basically, means to not be in a state in which one has lost their freedom of choice or action. So, let's introduce money here as well. One enters into a state of employment for the primary purpose of earning money. Why? To ally the fear of destitution. That being the case, employment could be considered just another form of indentured servitude which is just another form of slavery. Some might argue that this isn't true because of the existence of choice. If that's you, consider that since choice is simply a matter of forming a conclusion or judgement about a set of options and then carefully choosing the most suitable one...it ALWAYS exists. The presence of choice can't be a determining factor because there is always a choice.

Now we can see that freedom itself, within a society, is an illusion. Regardless what the of government or control structure exists, it remains something or something outside of the individual that is supposedly in a free state. If you have heard stories or "how to" examples of the sovereign man, you might come understanding that there is a way to escape the system. That may appear to be true but, in reality, by escaping one system you will end up as part of another system. Now, this part might sound insane but I'm telling you that all of these systems a part of one larger one. Think of them like rooms inside a large building. You can leave on room but by doing so you enter another. This happens over and over again. The only way out is to leave the building. The only way to leave the building is to die. This is best explained by taking a quick look at these rooms, these different forms of government.

Forms of Government

A government is the system or group of people having authority to conduct the policy, actions, and affairs of a state, organization, or people. Some people use terms like "Big Brother" to better describe the idea. This most often refers to a state. A state is a political organization with a centralized government that maintains a monopoly by the use of force within a certain geographical territory.

Yes, you read that correctly, the state maintains a monopoly by the use of force.

Let's rewind for a second and note that this meets all three descriptions of the word compulsion;

1. An irrational need or irresistible urge to perform some action, often despite negative consequences.
2. The use of authority, influence, or other power to force (compel) a person or persons to act.
3. The lawful use of violence (i.e. by the administration).

To force is to compel and governments do that lawfully. The only potential gray area might be the first description UNTIL one factors in politics and the political environment.

Once that is done, we are reminded of the examples streaming daily on CNN, FOX, MSNBC and the supposed "news" channels and we see first hand accounts of many of the irrational decisions that have and are being made despite the negative consequences purely out of a devotion to a political party.

Let's review some of the basic forms that government can take.

Autocracy - An autocracy is a system in which the highest capacity to influence the conduct of others is concentrated in the hands of one individual whose decisions aren't subject to outside legal restraints or popular public opinion except in the event of an overthrow. A monarchy is an example of an autocratic government.

Aristocracy - An aristocracy is similar to an autocracy except that rather than the power being consolidated under one person, it is consolidated under a ruling class of people. An oligarchy is an example of an aristocratic government.

Democracy - In a democracy, the entire voting population is involved in making decisions regarding the affairs of the state. The fact that the right to vote is not limited by wealth or race is the main point of distinction from other forms of government. In democracies, large proportions of the population may vote, either to make decisions or to choose representatives to make decisions. Political parties are common and significant in democracies. Political parties are groups of people with similar ideas about how a country or region should be run. Different political parties have different ideas about how the government should handle different problems. Democracy is the rule by the majority of the citizens.

Republic - When the country is considered a "public matter" rather than the private concern or property of the rulers and where offices of states are directly or indirectly elected or appointed rather than inherited, you have a republic. It gives rise to terms like, "Power to the People". This is because, in a republic, the people or some significant portion of the people have supreme control over the government and where offices of state are elected or chosen by elected people. A republic is rule by law.

These forms go government are just basic frameworks in that there are tons of variations creating new or hybrid forms that are base on the ones that I just mentioned. One thing that is common to each and every form of government that I just listed is that supreme power or control does not rest with the individual who is a part of the system that the government controls. In the case of an autocracy, an individual falls under the authority or rule of another individual. In the case of an aristocracy, an individual falls under the authority or rule of a small group of people. In the case of a democracy, an individual falls under the authority or rule of the majority of the citizens. In the case of a republic, an individual falls under the authority or rule of the law. In each and every case, an individual falls under the authority or rule of something else other than himself or herself. They are enslaved by a force outside of themselves.

One is not given the option of participation or non-participation at birth. It just is. There is no opting out. Once an individual reaches an age at which they can understand this and act against that force they are left with few choices, all leading to either similar or undesirable ends. One could rebel and face the possibility of destitution, detention, or violence. One could leave that state and simply fall under the authority or rule of another government under possibly worse conditions. One could leave that state and simply fall under the authority or rule of another state under similar or even better conditions (a better master). Or, one could choose to leave this physical existence altogether and fall under the rule or authority of no one.

If everyone thought this way, we would have a world full of angry and depressed people. Things just wouldn't work if everyone, or even too many people, began to think this way. How do we keep this from happening? We do that by understanding what it is that causes people to resist slavery in the first place.

People like to have control, especially in regards to their life. Having control means having choices. People need to feel like they have a choice.

Rats, Monkeys, Pigeons, and People

In her book The Art of Choosing, Sheena Iyengar refers to previous research and illustrates how choices define us and shape our lives regardless whether those choices seem mundane or life-altering at the time that we make them. In the book, pointing out research involving rats, monkeys, pigeons, and people in regards to their desire for and reactions to choices being offered to them, some observations were as follows;

Rats

Rats were given the option to choose between a direct path to a food source or a path to the food source that was littered with branches which required them to make choices along the way. The same type of food in the same amounts could be obtained by following either path. Logic would suggest that if the only goal was to obtain food, the rats would take the simplest path toward that end which, in this case, was the shorter, more direct, and unobstructed path. In contrast, the rats seemingly preferred the more indirect path and continuously chose that path.

Monkeys and Pigeons

In the experiments involving monkeys and pigeons, the animals learned that the behavior of pressing buttons enabled them to get food. If given a choice between a setup that featured one button and a different setup that featured multiple buttons, both monkeys and pigeons most often chose the setup with multiple buttons. This was the case even though the food obtained was of the same type and amount.

People

In research of the same type conducted with humans, the human test subjects were given chips to use at a casino. They were given the choice to either use the chips at a table that had one roulette wheel or to use the chips at a table where they could pick from two roulette wheels. Under this scenario, it was noted that people most often chose the table with two wheels, even though all of the wheels in the scenario were identical.

What does this tell us?

It tells us that, for the most part, animals (humans included) operate under the equation of choices = control = survival. Whether or not that expression is actually true, we tend to equate having choices with having control. Our instincts of survival tell us that the odds of us surviving increase with our level of control. We are constantly driven to seek control by our powerful unconscious minds and that desire causes us to continually seek choices.

Having choices because it makes us feel in control and we like that.

We won't always choose the fastest or efficient way of getting something done.

We want to feel that we are powerful and that we have choices.

It is because of this that the best way to get people to do the stuff you want them to do "willingly" and "freely" is to give them options. That way, they don't "feel" like a slave. Think about the case of sharecropping, the recently "freed" slaves had no desire to work under the labor gang style of work that they had done while in slavery but "chose" the sharecropper model because it didn't "feel" like slavery. They felt that they had a choice and, therefor, volunteered to be the means of production...the labor to generate money.

Choice and Fear

Want to hear something really weird about choice? I know you do so here goes… for a lot of people it is very important that they feel that they have choices in their lives. It makes them feel that they are in control. For this reason, some people will fight tooth and nail to defend their right to choose. At the same time, though, it seems that we actually have a lot less choice (and thus control) than we think we do and, interestingly enough, it could be in the most important areas of our lives that we have the least choice (and least control) of all.

Some choices, on the surface, seem to be pretty uncomplicated and easy to understand. On the other hand, some other choices are not really choices at all but, instead, are manipulative tactics used to encourage people to exhibit certain behaviors. For example, A construction leader might say to his followers "You have a choice. You can either finish stacking these materials now or you can come back after you take lunch and finish stacking it". This may have been presented as a choice but the real objective along with the coercive overtones, are clear.

If we ask "why" enough times, we'll uncover a truth that most (if not all) choices are driven by a basic fear. If we probe even further, we'll uncover a further truth that each and every one of these fears has a strong financial component.

Napoleon Hill, an author who became popular through his many different writings regarding success, exposed this when he wrote about "7 Basic Fears". The following are his words along with some of the financial concerns attached to those fears that I will add after each;

"7 Basic Fears"
by Napoleon Hill

Fear can be both a blessing and a curse, depending upon how and when one yields to it or rejects it.

The fear of failure can attract the causes of failure, and the fear of defeat is an open invitation for defeat. Fear is so powerful that it can do as much damage as its opposite-faith-can do good. As a matter of fact fear is nothing but faith in reverse gear.

There are seven basic fears which hold many people in bondage throughout their lives. No great and enduring success can be achieved by anyone until he has mastered all seven.

Fear of poverty: This fear is harbored by people who allow their minds to dwell on the circumstances and things they do not want. All thoughts have the habit of attracting to one the things one thinks about. This explains why one must condition his mind with a "success consciousness" before he can attract success. The emotions of faith and fear have equal pulling power-one attracts failure and the other attracts success as surely as water runs down hill in response to the law of gravitation.

The word "poverty" is synonymous with the word "destitution". Destitution, if you recall, means the scarcity or lack of a significant amount of material possessions or money. Destitution, specifically, refers to the complete lack of the means necessary to meet one's or one's families basic personal needs like food, clothing, and shelter. Two things can occur that can have a negative impact on one's future and subsequently that of others should this fear become too great. The first is as Mr. Hill stated, with their minds dwelling on the circumstances and things that they do not want (poverty in this case), they will attract more of the same to themselves. One could call that magical, spiritual, karmic, or any other word that they chose but the reality is that you can only think deeply about one thing at a time. If all of your time is spent thinking about what you do want, very little (if any) is spent figuring out how to get those things that you do want, The other thing that can occur bringing with it negative future outcomes or conditions is that if that poverty mindset is allowed to solidify and flourish, one can begin to support positions and efforts to transfer the responsibility for that away from oneself. You can find yourself supporting every position and cause that promises to be responsible for you, to take care of you financially. The trade-off is the relinquishing of more choice…more control…to become more deeply enslaved by a system.

Fear of criticism: The fear of what "they will say" of one's ideas or plans keeps millions of people from using their initiative in bringing forth ideas that could make them rich. And fear of criticism causes some minds to close up like clams, thereby depriving individuals of priceless opportunities to improve themselves by discovery of their weaknesses, mistakes, and poor judgment. The successful person invites criticism because he knows that it may reveal to him some advantage he had overlooked, or bring him some opportunity he had not expected.

This one is pretty much self-explanatory in a financial sense in that Mr. Hill clearly points out the missed financial opportunities that come from the fear of criticism. I would add that the criticism often extends to the money itself. Those who are a little short in the cash department often fear being criticized in that area creating a vicious financial cycle of not having and not pursuing because of not having.

Fear of ill health: Doctors have a sixty-four dollar word for this fear. It is hypochondria (imaginary illness). Here, the same as in connection with material things of a financial nature, the mind attracts that which it believes in, whether the belief is expressed through fear or by faith. Talking, thinking, and believing one is sick will bring about the effects of illness, and strangely enough, the symptoms appear to be the same as those which accompany real illness.

Slavery 2.0

Have you ever given any real thought to how expensive it can be to get sick. Your answer to that question is probably most dependent on two things; your age, and your health history. Anyone who has given ill health any modicum of thought is painfully aware of the costs associated with it. Most of them anyway. There are always a few surprises when that medical bill arrives. Entire industries thrive on this one fear alone raking in billions and billions of dollars each year. Mr. Hill mentions the mind attracting that which it believes in pointing out how much of the expenditures regarding health and wellness are for illegitimate reasons resulting from simple thought. The other end of that spectrum is the tons of money being made from medical equipment manufacturers, the pharmaceutical industry, health gurus, etc. The financial impact to the the economy is massive. Depending on how you look at it, the financial impact on the individual can be seen more so.

A recent Gallup poll points out how Americans are strained and fear ballooning healthcare costs. At the same time, according to the poll, 64% say they are "completely" or "mostly" satisfied with their personal experience of the healthcare system. That sounds great but how does it match up with these numbers; one in four skipped a medical treatment because of cost, and in the past year alone, Americans collectively borrowed an estimated $88 billion to cover healthcare costs. That sounds like a pretty substantial financial burden. I would guess that it was substantial enough to be a huge part of the decision making process of the average person, wouldn't you?

Think about these three things:

• 45% of U.S. adults are concerned that a major health event could lead to bankruptcy.
• U.S. adults borrowed an estimated $88 billion in the past year to cover medical costs.
• Republicans consider the quality of care in the U.S. to be among the best in the world to the tune of 67% while only 38% of Democrats agree.

Now, having thought about that, ask yourself how much that affects the choices one has and is willing to choose; and then how the choices selected impacted the level of freedom one really has as a result. I think most would choose to be (what they perceive as) more secure and lose freedom and control as a result. An added effect is that, as a member of this society, you get to fall under whatever resulting rules, regulation, or laws that are produced by whatever form of government exists. Is that freedom or slavery, there is no in between.

Fear of the loss of love: This is the fear which causes jealousy. Not infrequently it leads to both temporary and permanent insanity. Whether it is justified or not, jealousy destroys homes, breaks up business and professional relationships, and leads to physical ailments on a scale scarcely equaled by any of the other fears. It has been said that women are more susceptible to the fear of jealousy than men are, due perhaps to their knowledge of the polygamous nature of the male.

One of the reasons that women can feel the way that they do when it comes to jealousy is that the implications of promiscuity and extra-marital affairs go far beyond simple heartbreak. It has often been said that, in terms of what each partner historically brought to a relationship, the woman's value was large derived from her beauty and ability to bear children while the man's value was largely derived from his ability to provide. Again we enter into the world of money. If a man was to cheat on a woman, she might find that hard enough to swallow by itself but I've heard (on many occasions) women express that if the man diverted resources to the other women (spent money on her) that made the situation much much worse. What if there was a child produced as a result of the affair? Financial resources would have to be diverted from her use and benefit to that of the outside child, and that child's mother.

Coming from the masculine perspective, this fear of the loss of love manifests itself financially all too often mostly due to the fact that, in a committed relationship, the male usually sustains a hefty financial blow upon the failure of the relationship. This is above and beyond the financial sacrifices and contributions he had made up until that point in attempting to "prove himself" in the first place.

Fear of the loss of liberty: Every human being has a deeply seated and inborn desire for freedom, a gift perhaps by the Creator who gave man complete rights to use his mind-power as a means of providing himself with freedom to work out his own earthly destiny. This is the only one of the seven basic fears which is founded upon circumstances over which the individual does not have the power of control. With the world in the state of chaos and frustration existing today there is ample reason to justify one's fear of losing his liberty.

The fear of the loss of liberty has at least one direct correlation to money in that one could actually lose what liberty that they do have, and become imprisoned, for not having it. This is what occurs in the case of debt bondage. As previously discussed, debt bondage is the pledge of a person's services as security for the repayment for a debt or other obligation. Out of convenience and also for the purpose of obscuring the meaning, the following conditions are often added;

- where the terms of the repayment are not clearly or reasonably stated
- the person who is holding the debt and thus has some control over the laborer, does not intend to ever admit that the debt has been repaid.
- The services required to repay the debt may be undefined,
- the services' duration may be undefined, thus allowing the person supposedly owed the debt to demand services indefinitely.
- Debt bondage can be passed on from generation to generation.

One must then ask an important question of clarity. If the follow on conditions are not present but a person's services have been pledged as security for the repayment for a debt or other obligation, what is that called?

If you notice, each of the follow on conditions has an undefined effect on time. Time is the unknown factor. That being said, the condition is the same while that state exists and isn't that what is most important?

Isn't that what makes it what it is?

Would temporary slavery still be slavery even though it was called by another name?

Fear of old age: Just why men and women should curtail their usefulness because of their fear of old age is difficult to define. For it's obvious that the Creator has so wisely provided man with everything he needs, with which to work out his earthly existence, 'that nothing can be taken away from him without something of equal or greater value becoming available to take its place. As one gives up his youth, its place is filled by wisdom. And history proves that man's greatest achievements take place after he passes the half-century mark. Moreover, age is not accurately measured by the years one has lived, but it is determined by the nature of the thinking he does and his reactions to his experiences.

Mr. Hill brings up a great point regarding the fact that it is often after they reach middle age that men make their greatest achievements. Many people feel that as they age they become less and less useful and thusly less capable of making money. In addition to that, a huge financial concern is whether or not the nest egg that they have managed to build is going to be big enough to carry them through their retirement years. After all, what is the thing that is necessary to make retirement an enjoyable and permanent condition? An adequate predictable income stream is what can make their retirement years both enjoyable and permanent. Without that, it will either not be as enjoyable as it should have been or, even worse, disrupted by the need to rejoin the workforce in order to make ends meet.

Making this fear even worse is the sad fact that most people either don't understand how money works or don't have enough of knowledge about how money works to make money work for them as hard and as long as it could. Some people have a slight understanding of the impact that inflation and taxation have on their portfolio, enough of an understanding to cause them stress and worry about aging but not enough of an understanding of how to allay those fears, at least to a significant degree.

Fear of death: This is the grandfather of all of the seven basic fears, and the most unnecessary of them all because it is something over which no one has enduring control. One man who mastered this fear explained how he did it this way: "I believed" said he, "that death brings one or the other of two conditions. Either it results in one long, eternal sleep, or it carries us to another world far superior to the one we leave behind, and neither of these possibilities is terrifying."

Death would seem to be the last thing that one would have to fear in terms of finances but that really isn't the case. The fear of death itself is understandable because it equates to the fear of the unknown. No one has been given evidence as to what lies beyond the veil of death. Naturally, the presence of doubt gives way to fear. But financially, the fears come from the conditions that others who are important to us may face rather than what we may face when we pass on.

Along with our dying, typically, comes the death of our income and income producing ability. The result of this could mean the survivors moving from one economic class to another or even not having the basic necessities that are needed in life. Over time, we can become so accustomed to the way things are that we forget how easily they can change. A little financial repositioning can result in a huge lifestyle change.

How often do we see situations in which a married couple is heavily dependent on the income of one of the two and the other, sadly, has no capacity to continue the activities that produced that income upon the death of the other?

How often do we see situations in which there is no safety net in place that can provide financial protection should one (or both) of the parents pass away while the children are still unable to fend for themselves, financially?

Looking beyond the immediate and obvious impacts that an unprepared for and unexpected death can reap on a family, imagine the long term financial impacts that a lack of knowledge can have on the heirs and generations to come. The system, by design, is designed to dismantle and absorb the wealth of those who have passed on if proper steps have not been taken beforehand to protect it.

The seven basic fears as Napoleon Hill listed listed them (fear of poverty, fear of criticism, fear of ill-health, fear of the loss of love, fear of the loss of liberty, fear of old age, and fear of death) all have a financial component that, in attempts to manage, causes people to make decisions that they would not otherwise make if money wasn't involved. In a sense, money doesn't only alter reality, it actually creates a new one.

Governmental Fear Protection

A DIRECT CORRELATION BETWEEN SECURITY AND FREEDOM

The size and scale of the government of the United States of America continues to grow and grow along with the power that the government yields. It's amazing that, in a country that touts freedom as its origins, continues to transfer more and more power away from the people and continues consolidating that power at the state and federal level. Along with that is the requirement for more and more tax revenue to generate the funding to feed this massive juggernaut. It doesn't really make a lot of sense, at first glance, until one recognizes the driving force behind it. The driving force behind the government's growth and continued power grabs is fear.

America, being a republic, is a nation of laws. To put it more precisely, America is founded upon the principle of the rule of law. This principle states that all people and institutions are subject to and accountable to law that is fairly applied and enforced. Government, in the case of the United States is based on laws. This can be a very good thing since it protects the population from a many of the injustices that can exist in a country that is ruled by one or only a few people. The law, having been developed within a fair, just, and equatable (in theory) process, is there to protect us. A good question to ask is whether the law is there to protect the rights of everyone or just most of us. A broad answer to that question would be that the law exists to protect the many…not all.

An example of what I mean by this would be in the case of laws created to either protect the life of an unborn child or to protect the rights of an expectant mother. If a law is created to protect the life of an unborn child, the effect is the limiting of the rights of the expecting mother to decide whether or not she wants to carry the child to full term. On the other hand, if a law is created to protect the right of an expecting mother to terminate the pregnancy at will, the right of the child to live is taken away. This is but one example of the duality of the rule of law when it comes to the rights of people. There are thousands of others.

What is the effect of this duality when it comes to fear?

If we keep in mind that laws are created for the protection of the many, it becomes much easier to see how broad this effect can be. With a goal of creating new laws that abridge the freedoms of some, one has to simply manipulate the fears of the many. But doing so, new laws will be passed at the behest of the constituency and according to the desire of those in the political positions to get those laws passed. Since America is a nation of laws imposing the rule of law, the government is not only inclined to but also required to enforce those laws. In order to enforce those laws, either new organizations or departments within the government must be created or existing ones must be expanded.

The creation of the Department of Homeland Security provides an excellent example of how government is expanded on the basis of fear. The Homeland Security Act created the United States Department of homeland Security in 2002 in the aftermath of the terrorist attacks on U.S. soil on September 11th, 2001. There was also a new cabinet-

Governmental Fear Protection

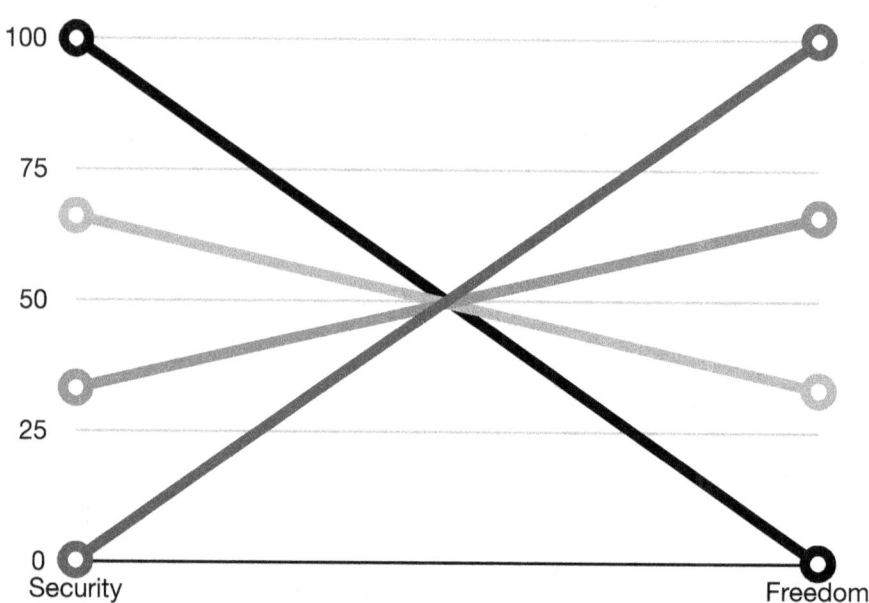

level position created as part of this Act. It was the largest federal government reorganization since the Department of Defense was created by the National Security Act of 1947. What was the driving force behind the creation of the department, fear, plain and simple. Because the level of fear was so high and fueled by political rhetoric and the media, it was easy for the powers that be to make this happen with the support of much, if not most, of the American public. This was governmental fear protection at its finest.

The other side of the coin that doesn't get much focus is that of the "freedoms" that were restricted or diminished as a result of this move. Make no mistake, freedom and security are polar opposites. If you want to increase protection, you must decrease freedom. If you want to increase freedom, you must decrease security. There is simply no way around this. If you wanted to grant your child more freedom by allowing them to go outside and play, you must accept (and consider) the fact that the level of protection has decreased by exposing them to the dangers of being outside of the home. So, in essence, if you want the government to protect you, you have to accept and consider the fact that it must have more control to do this. The result is the reduction of your freedom. Oddly enough, most Americans never really question whether or not that which they feared really truly existed. An additional, and huge, consequence was that the size and scope of the government was increased substantially.

More Security Equals Less Freedom

Consider the words of Senator Ron Paul (R-TX) in November of 2002.

> *The administration and Congress put the finishing touches on the monstrous Homeland Security bill last week, creating the first new federal department since the Department of Defense at the end of World War II. Laughably, the new department has been characterized as merely a "reorganization" of existing agencies, even though I notice no department was abolished to make up for it! One thing we can be sure of in this world is that federal agencies grow. The*

Homeland Security department, like all federal agencies, will increase in size exponentially over the coming decades. Its budget, number of employees, and the scope of its mission will EXPAND. Congress has no idea what it will have created twenty or fifty years hence, when less popular presidents have the full power of a domestic spying agency at their disposal.

The frightening details of the Homeland Security bill, which authorizes an unprecedented level of warrantless spying on American citizens, are still emerging. Those who still care about the Bill of Rights, particularly the 4th amendment, have every reason to be alarmed. But the process by which Congress created the bill is every bit as reprehensible as its contents.

Ironically, many in Congress who usually champion limited government were enthusiastic supporters of the largest federal expansion in 50 years. Twenty years ago President Reagan revitalized conservatives across the country by appealing to their Goldwater roots, promising to slash the size of government and eliminate whole departments. Yet the promise of a smaller government went unfulfilled, and today Congress passes budgets even larger that those of the Clinton years.

Of course the Homeland Security bill did receive some opposition from the President's critics. Yet did they attack the legislation because it threatens to debase the 4th amendment and create an Orwellian surveillance society? Did they attack it because it will chill political dissent or expand the drug war? No, they attacked it on the grounds that it failed to secure enough high-paying federal union jobs, thus angering one of Washington's most powerful special interest groups. Ultimately, however, even the most prominent critics voted for the bill.

The lesson learned from the rush to create a Homeland Security department is that the size and scope of government grows regardless of which party is in power. The federal government now devours a whopping 40% of the nation's GDP, the highest level since World War II – and a massive new department can only make things worse. The Homeland Security bill provides a vivid example of the uncontrolled spending culture in Washington, a culture that views the true source of political power – your tax dollars – as unlimited.

If you recall the earlier chapter regarding taxation, you know that the creation of a larger government requires either the increase or the reallocation of the taxes imposed on you.

Which of the two do you believe is more likely?
An increase of the tax burden, for whatever reason, restricts freedoms in one way or another. In effect, increasing your level of indenture…slavery.

Governmental Fear Protection

Political Party Influence

Political party influences have been a dominate factor in the area of slavery since they came into being in the United States. This influence grew as the eventual "abolishment" of slavery in this country neared. Although, on the surface, it may have appeared that the parties held opposing views as to the need for slavery to exist, it is more accurate to state that the political parties held opposing views as to the form of slavery that should exist in America. Remember, slavery has not and can not be abolished in the United Staes of America. The only things that changes is the choices that exist pertaining to it.

The political spectrum in the United States is dominated by two political parties; the Democratic Party and the Republican Party. Every United States presidential election since 1852 has been won by one of these two parties and they have controlled the United States Congress, for the most part, since 1856. Interestingly, the United States constitution makes no references to political parties; there were no political parties at the time that it came into existence.

Isn't it funny how both political parties constantly make references to the Constitution while that document never even addressed their necessity or authorized them?

This modern two-party system also includes several "third parties", the largest of which is the Libertarian Party.

Between the two major parties, you can see an almost dance-like interaction with either party taking control from time to time and then that control shifting back to the other party at different times. The result of this dance, typically, is more power placed in the hands of the government. One can see, by observing with an open-mind, that it really isn't so much about government control (or lack thereof) so much as it is about "what" the government controls and regulates in the united States. Both parties take very different positions in this area.

The Democratic Party

The Democratic Party was founded as the Democratic-Republican party in 1792 by Thomas Jefferson and James Madison, it is the older of the two major political parties in the United States.

Both Thomas Jefferson and James Madison owned were slave owners.

At the time that it was founded, the Democratic Party was the prevailing party among white southerners and was then the party most associated with the pro-slavery position. Later, the party has successfully positioned itself as the liberal party regarding domestic issues. Some of the things that the party supports includes;

Social Justice

A concept of a fair and just relationship between the individual and the society. Measurements for that belief include wealth, opportunities for personal activity, and social privileges. This is mainly rooted in emphasis on barrier breaking in regards to social mobility (movement of people within or between social classes), the creation of safety nets, and economic justice.Social justice is about individuals receiving what is due to them from society.

Social Liberalism

A certain ethical set of principles or values, doctrines, myths, or symbols explaining that society should work in a manner that includes a regulated free market economy along with the expansion of civil rights. Within this framework, the government is expected to address economic and social issues such as poverty, health care, and education.

Mixed Economy

An economic system that "mixes" parts of market economies (supply and demand) with certain ideas regarding planned economies (economy-wide economic and production plans). Another feature of a mixed economy is a wide use of state intervention and regulatory oversight. Various definitions of "mixed economy" exist.

Welfare State

A form of government in which the state protects and promotes the economic and social well-being of the citizens resulting in the state, essentially, being responsible for their welfare. It is based on equitable distribution of wealth, and public responsibility for citizens who are unable to care for themselves and obtain the basics required for a "good life"

So, in order for this stated mission of the Democratic Party to be successful, the government must have the power to compel individuals and businesses to contribute financially to the means necessary for these things to happen. To facilitate that, the more power that is placed in the hands of the government to compel people to do the aforementioned, the better.

The Republican Party

The Republican Party was founded in 1854 by northern anti-slavery activists and modernizers and, although younger than the Democratic Party, was nicknamed the "Grand Ole Party" or GOP. Abraham Lincoln was the first member of the Republican Party to be elected as President of the United States. Of the two major political parties, the Republican Party has been the more market oriented parties with a platform that supports; economic liberalism, fiscal conservatism, and social conservatism.

Economic Liberalism

An economic system in which emphasis is placed on the greatest number of economic decisions being made by individuals or households rather than by collective institutions or organizations. Within the theory of economic liberalism, strong support can be seen for a market economy (supply and demand) and private property (non-governmental ownership) of the means of production.

Fiscal Conservatism

A political-economic philosophy regarding the use of government revenue collection (primarily taxes) and spending to monitor and influence the economy along with a budget in which revenues are equal to expenditures. Fiscal conservatism advocates low taxes, reduced government spending, and minimal government debt. Four of the defining qualities of fiscal conservatism are; free trade, economic deregulation, lower taxes, and privatization. This is in contrast with welfare state and expanded regulatory policies associated with liberalism following the New Deal.

Social Conservatism

The belief that society is built upon a fragile network of relationships which need to be upheld through duty, traditional values, and established institutions. One trait of social conservatism is that it is skeptical, for the most part, of social change. Another is the belief in maintaining the status quo in social areas such as family life, sexual relations, and patriotism. Much of the rise of social conservatism in North America can be credited to a reactionary response to federal action on social issues like the rights of Lesbian, Gays, Transgenders, and Transvestites (LGBT) and abortion issues.

The Republican Party tends to have the most influence in the states in the southern united States as well as in states between the east and west coasts of the country "flyover states", generally referring to the part of the country that many Americans only view by air when traveling and never actually see in person at ground level.

The Libertarian Party

Founded in 1971, the Libertarian Party is the largest continuing political party in the United States. Its stated sore mission is to reduce the size, influence, and expenditures of all levels of government. For these reasons, the Libertarian Party supports the following;

Minimal market regulation equaling minimal government involvement and interference resulting in a strongly supply and demand driven economy.

A less powerful federal government resulting in more power and decision making ability being left to the individual states and the individual citizens.

Strong civil liberties creating and protecting personal guarantees and freedoms that the government cannot abridge, either by law or by legal interpretation, without due process.

Drug liberalization promoting the process of eliminating or reducing drug prohibition laws.

Separation of church and state defining and maintaining the political distance in the relationship between. Religious organization and the nation state along with a change to the existing formal relationship between the church and the state within the United States of America.

Open immigration promoting the idea that people should be able to migrate to and from whatever country they choose.

Non-interventionism and neutrality in diplomatic relations promoting a foreign policy that minimizes relations with other nations while maintaining diplomacy and trade along with neutrality in war amongst other countries.

Free trade promoting a trade policy in which there is no restriction on imports or exports to and from the United States.

A summary of the   Libertarian Party stance is that Libertarianism is the view that each person has the right to live his life in any way he chooses so long as he respects the equal rights of others. Libertarians defend each person's right to life, liberty, and property-rights that people have naturally, before governments are created.

Political Party Games

Since "Third Parties" in the political spectrum have little power and influence in in the grand scheme of things, most the political games that shape and form the power structure within the United States of America are played between the two major political parties and, in a sense, on the people who live there. In fact, the outcomes of these games have a serious impact on the world, as a whole. Always remember that others often have no problem whatsoever infringing on your freedoms if it makes them feel better about their condition or for the sake of their beliefs.

"The only freedom which deserves the name is that of pursuing our own good in our own way, so long as we do not attempt to deprive others of theirs, or impede their efforts to obtain it. Each is the proper guardian of his own health, whether bodily, or mental or spiritual. Mankind are

greater gainers by suffering each other to live as seems good to themselves, than by compelling each to live as seems good to the rest."

— John Stuart Mill (On Liberty)

Although this writing is not intended to be political, I would be remiss if I did not include a reference to the impact that the shifts of power between the political parties has on the actual and perceived "freedoms" of the people of the United States. Both parties have separate and different stated objectives but one important fact remains. In order to implement each of their agendas, it is necessary to implement rules, regulations, and laws that compel the population to adhere to the guidelines that are set forth upon implementation. These rules, regulations and laws all have an impact on individual freedoms in every sense of the word. Recall these definitions from earlier in this book;

Freedom Definition 1 - *The power or right to act, speak, or think a one wants without hindrance or restraint.*

Increasing rules and regulations directly impact the individuals right to act, speak, or think as that individual wants without hindrance or restraint. Some laws put into place are designed specifically to do just that.

Freedom Definition 2 - Absence of subjection to foreign domination or despotic government.

Increasing rules and regulations increase the power of the government, regardless of the intention, individual power is reduced as there is a direct and inverse relationship between government and individual power.

Freedom Definition 3 - The state of not being imprisoned or enslaved.

Increasing rules and regulations put into place, regardless of their intention, increasingly individual freedoms and choices of action.

By dangling objectives in front of voters that seemingly coincide with that voters ideal an opportunity is created to consolidate more power at the government level. Individuals have a tendency to give up that power quickly and willingly when the decision that is put forth coincides with their personal opinions and desires never considering that the execution of that objective and the implementation of that law increases the power of the government (whether directly or indirectly) transferring that power away from the individual.

The political party that openly recognizes this and addresses this is the Libertarian Party which, ironically, boasts the least influence and power in the political arena.

War

We see and hear about it all the time, war. It is often characterized as a struggle between the good guys and the bad guys. In these cases, there is an overarching idea about some noble causes necessitating the need for heroes to gather and rise up against this opposing force. For example, terms such as "The Axis of Evil". Can you tell who the bad guys were? I'm sure that they didn't see themselves that way. In any case, there is a noble cause established requiring the populace to rise up against this enemy that has come (or is coming) to steal, kill, and to destroy. Feeling justified in their cause, atrocities are often committed by both the "bad guys" and "good guys". Who the good guys are and who the bad guys are depends on who you ask. The reason for war also depends on who you ask. Sometimes, it really isn't about the "good guys" and the "bad guys". Sometimes, the best way to truly understand the reasons for going to war is to understand the real meaning of the word.

War can be defined as a state of armed conflict between states, governments, and societies and informal paramilitary groups such as mercenaries, insurgents, and militias. That pretty much covers the definition but what about the meaning? The meaning of a word can often be more telling as to its true nature. The origins of the English word "war" can be traced back to Old Saxon and Old High German words meaning "to confuse", "to perplex", and "to bring into confusion".

That's the key word here, "confusion".

Most often, war and the economy are deeply connected with quite a few of them being either partially based or entirely based on economic reasons. Some economists believe that war can have the overall effect of stimulating a nation's economy. It is also commonly believed that the general population, in most cases, don't want war and must be manipulated in order to support it. The following is a quote by Hermann Göring (Nazi military and political leader) at the Nurmberg trials following World War II that artfully exposes intentionally confusing the populace (as to the true reasons for war) as common practice regarding the initiation of war;

Naturally, the common people don't want war; neither in Russia nor in England nor in America, nor for that matter in Germany. That is understood. But, after all, it is the leaders of the country who determine the policy and it is always a simple matter to drag the people along, whether it is a democracy or a fascist dictatorship or a Parliament or a Communist dictatorship. ... the people can always be brought to the bidding of the leaders. That is easy. All you have to do is tell them they are being attacked and denounce the pacifists for lack of patriotism and exposing the country to danger. It works the same way in any country.

Was he right?

I believe that he was.

I believe that the reason for war is and has always been about resources. It always occurs as either an attempt to secure more resources or to manipulate an economy in some way, shape, or form. It's always about the money. Let me give you an example of why I believe this to be the case.

The Iraq war was deemed necessary based on a claim the Iraq and its leader, Saddam Hussein, was harboring "weapons of mass destruction" making them a threat to the security of America and the rest of the world. Weapons were indeed found, chemical weapons, and they were so old that the chances of them being used as they were designed to be used were slim. There was no Weapons of Mass Destruction (WMD) program uncovered either. What is interesting, though, is that Saddam Hussein had attempted to switch from the petrodollar in the oil trade and to sell Iraqi oil in exchange for other currencies or commodities. A petrodollar is a notional unit of currency earned by a country from the export of petroleum and it is pegged to the United States Dollar. Even more interesting is the fact that, following the Iraq war and the subsequent removal of Saddam Hussein, Iraq returned the denomination of its oil sales to the US Dollar, despite the fact that the dollar had fallen in value.

It was all about the money.

An Unescapable System (Matrix)

LEARN THE RULES AND THEN BEND THEM TO YOUR WILL

No matter which way we turn, there is no escaping the system in which we live. It is a world-wide system spanning the whole of the earth and compelling all who live upon it to participate in it in some form or another whether they want to or not. This is the point in which some reading this might say, "Ha! There is no choice! This is one situation where a person cannot choose!" To that, I would respond that there is always a choice, even in this. Unfortunately, the choice that would completely extricated a person from this system is death. The system exercises control through at least three major mechanisms; Many, Religion, and Politics.

Money

This mechanism requires little further explanation as a good portion of this book has been dedicated to explaining the influence of money. Just about all, if not all, decisions that are made on every level have a financial component. Where we live and how we live are influenced by money. What job we choose and what employer we choose to do that job for are influenced by money. Even when we decide to base our decisions on a "higher purpose" money remains a concerns and influences that decision in some way or another. There is no escape, save death.

Religion

Let me start by elaborating on the definition of religion. While most might define religion as the belief in and worship of a a superhuman controlling power, especially a personal God or gods, a more broad definition is simply that of a system of faith and worship. Although we would like to believe that religion is the key to escaping the matrix. Almost every religion that I have come into contact with carries with it a promise of an eventual escape from this earthly realm and its systems of control. As we've seen already, it is religion that is actually a very large part of keeping people in line with this system. One could debate from sun up until sun down as to whether or not religion is a good or bad thing but that is not the point. What we have to focus on in order to truly understand are the choices and outcomes that are made right here on earth that influence an individuals rights and abilities to make their own choices. Slavery, in a traditional sense has been condoned by religion over and over again. Slavery in a different sense continues to be heavily influenced by religion in ways that most people are completely unaware.

Politics

Politics are defined as the activities associated with the governance of a country or other area, especially the debate or conflict among individuals or parties having or hoping to achieve power. Basically, it comes down to who gets what, when they get it, and how they get it. The concept manifests itself on different levels. On the formal level, politics refer to the operation of government on a large scale causing most people to view it as something outside of themselves. Semi-formal politics refer to government on a small scale such as that of neighborhood associations and student governments, some continue to maintain the view of an outsider in these settings. Perhaps, the most important level of politics for the individual is that of in-formal politics which is understood as the forming of alliances, exercising power, and protecting and advancing ideas or goals. The latter can include anything affecting ones daily life. Some examples of informal politics are the way an office or household is managed or how one person or group exercises influence over another. Simply put, politics is everywhere.

Where can we go where money, religion, or politics do not affect us? Where can we go where these three factors don't shape our physical environment in ways that directly affect our choices? On a deeper level, we can see that what appears as three separate mechanisms within a system, are all so deep interwoven that there is no way to separate the second and third from the first. Every religious institution, in order to function, requires a source of money to use to work toward its ends. Every political structure is in need of and heavily influenced by money. As we established earlier, money is the driving force behind slavery. These three mechanisms in combination are the forces behind slavery in its various forms as well as the influences that cause it change its shape and form seeming to disappear at times but never ever really going away.

With that being said, shouldn't money be the answer?

Doesn't everything that we have discussed up until this point amount to "financial slavery"?

If money can enslave us, shouldn't it be able to do the opposite?

Can't money be our ticket to freedom?

Money, no doubt, in sufficient quantities would go a long way toward providing us with more choices. What are the forces working agains that end?

Financial Freedom

A common and accepted definition of financial freedom is that if you have enough more stored away, money in other places making you more money, and enough cash to spend on the things that you need and want…you have attained financial freedom. With that financial freedom, we are free to retire from working or, alternatively, pursue a career that suits our liking rather than being forced to consider how much we will be earning in that career. What I find interesting is that every part of that definition includes a need for money. How can you be free of something that you need? Isn't it kind of like saying "food freedom" or "clothing freedom" or "shelter freedom"?

A simplistic view of financial freedom would be that if we can earn enough money, we can be free. A common view of financial freedom is that if we are to earn enough money to gain financial freedom, it will take time… a long time. This is why the idea of retirement down the road is so appealing. It encompasses both views, earning enough money and being free at a certain time to live our lives as we truly desire. The idea, itself, makes sense but it opens the door to two very important questions;

How much money will it take to be financially free?

And

How much time will it take to be financially free?

In order to know the answers to these questions, we need to know how money works and, unless you were born with all of the money that you will ever need, you have to (as the master) know what needs to be done with what you own and to take the required actions to get there!

1. Know where your slaves are and what they are doing.

You have to pay very close attention to where your money is and what it is doing. Every once in a while it is necessary to inspect your slaves which will allow you to better manage their activities. Knowing that there are more of them than there are of you and that you can't be in more than one place at a time, you must use the tools available to you to accomplish this. The slave masters of old had to physically move around their properties to do this (or have someone else do it) but thankfully you have the internet and technology to help you keep a watchful eye on your slaves.

2. Increase the number of slaves working for you.

Every slave that remains on your plantation and under your control is a slave that can continue to work for you. That means that every dollar that is not spent is money on your pocket. That money can be used toward paying off your debts and acquiring more wealth. Another option is to explore the possibility of finding a higher paying job or additional part-time work. You can also make adjustments to the allowances on your W-2 if you normally get a tax refund allowing you to keep that money working for you rather than the government all year.

3. Eliminate debt.

Consider consolidating your debt when it can be done to help you pay the debt of sooner and with less money overall. This can help you free up additional cash to pay higher interest loans off and become debt free sooner. You want your slaves working for you and not someone else because the only time it makes sense to hire them out is when you earn more that way than if they were working on your property.

4. Build an emergency fund.

Keep a few slaves in reserve to go to work in case of an emergency without disrupting the work that you are doing to build your financial independence. As a general rule, you should keep 3 - 6 months of income or salary in reserve where it can be accessed if there is an emergency.

5. Protect what is yours.

When you are younger, the primary concern is protecting your income. You can accomplish this by having insurance that will replace the income in the event of death or disability. Think of it as insuring the work of your slaves in the event they are prevented from producing for you for any reason. When you are older, the primary concern is protecting your assets. You can accomplish that by having insurance that will replace the loss of your possessions. Think of it as insuring the lives of your slaves themselves.

6. Win the two battles of financial independence.

If you want to gain your financial independence and live life on your terms, financially, there are two battles that must be won.

Can I be strong with you?

If you don't win both of these battles, the chances of you ever gaining financial independence are slim to none (and slim just left the building).

The two battles that you must win are the battle of inflation and the battle of taxes. We know that taxes aren't so much about how much you make as it is about what you keep, we'll talk about that shortly. For now, let's talk about inflation.

What is inflation?

Have you ever heard of the Rule of 72?

The Rule of 72 is was put forth by Albert Einstein and what it amounts to is a simple way for us to determine about how long it would take your money to double at a given interest rate. The way that this works is by taking the interest rate that you are earning on your money and dividing that into 72, the result is how long it would take (in years) for your money to double. For example, if you were getting a 4% return on your money; you would divide 4 into 72 and the result would be 18. So, at a 4% return on your money, it would take 18 years for your money to double.

Let's say you had $100 and you were getting a 4% return on it.

By using the Rule of 72, we know that 18 years later we would have $200.

18 years after that, we would have $400.

So, in 36 years, your $100 dollars would have grown into $400.

But the question is will $400 dollars buy you what $100 will buy you today…36 years from now.

That is inflation.

A lot of people might answer "no" to the question right away but others might have to think about. If you have to think about it, a good question to ask yourself is if you have to think about it, how much has your money really grown? As a point of reference, I'll share the story of my cell phone with you. It wasn't that long ago that a cellphone could be had for around $200. I recently had to replace my phone and it cost me over $800. While I was there shopping for a new phone, I saw that there were even phones there that cost upwards of $1000. It hasn't taken anywhere close to 36 years for the price of a cellphone to go up over 400%. It probably hasn't even been half that time.

Inflation is the reduction of spending power of your money over time.

If you want to win the battle of inflation, your money has to grow faster (preferably much faster) than inflation is reducing its spending power.

Let's say we take a 29 year old who is aware of the need and wants to save money for his or her retirement. They take $10,000 and put it away earning a 4% return on their money. They don't add to it and they don't take anything from it.

18 years later, at age 47, their money would have increased to $20,000.

18 years later, at age 65, their money would have increased to $40,000.

A total of 36 years have passed and now they have reached their expected age of retirement with a total of $40,000 in their retirement account.

Imagine this is you and the time has come for you to live life on your terms. You've retired from your job and you are now ready to spend time traveling the world, visiting with and spending time with your grandchildren, or just doing the things that you always wanted to but never had time to do before. Bearing in mind that you've just given up a huge chunk of the income that you had coming in while you were working, how long would that $40,000 last?

If you're like most people, you could go through that in a year or less. Now, you're 66 years old and you're dead broke, what do you do? You get a job (Just Over Broke). You go back to work and give up the "freedom" you have been waiting all of those years for so that you can have some money in your pocket.

Now, think about the same $10,000 investment except instead of getting a 4% return on your money, you get a 12% return on it, What would that look like?

By following the Rule of 72, we take 12 and divide it into 72. The result is 6. So, now we know that at a 12% interest rate of return, your money would double every 6 years.

You put that same $10,000 away at age 29 at a 12% interest rate and don't touch it.

Instead of your money doubling once in 18 years, your money would double 3 times in the same amount of time.

18 years later, at age 47, your money would have increased to $80,000.

18 years later, at age 65, your money would have increased to $640,000.

Isn't that amazing?

That's a $600,000 difference and the only thing that you changed was the interest rate. There are a lot of moving parts in this example but in order for anything like this to happen, you would have to do two things; you would have to start early and you would have to be firm in your investment.

It's been said that there are two things that are certain in this life, death and taxes. Taxes can take a huge chunk out of your ability to save money building your army of slaves. Make sure that you understand all of the tax advantages that are available to you and use them to reduce the amount of money that you have to turn over to the government.

7. Plan for generational wealth

Not having an estate plan in place can cost you plenty when it comes to providing for your family's future should you leave the game. Everything that you have spent your life building can be destroyed if you don't have a good plan in place. The choices that you make regarding estate plan will play a major role in whether your children become masters or either became or remain financially enslaved.

Sadly, this is not something that we learn in school. That would be in direct opposition to the mental slavery that prevails in our society. In fact, that is the very reason that most people will never experience financial freedom in their lifetime.

Mental Slavery

Slavery in America, a more recent occurrence provides us with an example the process of enslaving the mind. Slavery, as previously discussed, has not been abolished. It has merely been transformed. Even still, the steps necessary to foster the slave mentality in an individual remain rudimentarily the same. Slavery is a mindset. To make a slave, one must either alter the mindset of the intended victim by removing the thoughts of freedom to the extent possible and replacing that mindset with one of submission. How is that accomplished? It is accomplished through instilling the mindsets consistent with low self esteem, powerlessness, and a lack of free will.

A speech detailing a method for doing this gave rise to a condition known as Willie Lynch Syndrome. This speech was supposedly delivered by a white slave owner, William Lynch in 1712, however in recent years, both White and Black historians have argued that this was not the case claiming dates and events cannot be verified. Nevertheless, I thought it helpful to include the letter due to my belief that behaviors being witnessed today still (heavily) coincide with statements made in the letter. The following is the letter in its entirety.

Slavery 2.0

Gentlemen, I greet you here on the bank of the James River in the year of our Lord one thousand seven hundred and twelve. First, I shall thank you, the gentlemen of the Colony of Virginia, for bringing me here. I am here to help you solve some of your problems with slaves. Your invitation reached me on my modest plantation in the West Indies, where I have experimented with some of the newest and still the oldest methods for control of slaves. Ancient Rome would envy us if my program is implemented. As our boat sailed south on the James River, named for our illustrious King, whose version of the Bible we cherish, I saw enough to know that your problem is not unique. While Rome used cords of wood as crosses for standing human bodies along its highways in great numbers, you are here using the tree and the rope on occasion.

I caught the whiff of a dead slave hanging from a tree a couple miles back. You are not only losing valuable stock by hangings, you are having uprisings, slaves are running away, your crops are sometimes left in the fields too long for maximum profi t, you suffer occasional fi res, your animals are killed. Gentlemen, you know what your problems are; I do not need to enumerate your problems, I am here to introduce you to a method of solving them. In my bag here, I have a fool proof method for controlling your black slaves, I guarantee everyone of you that if installed correctly will control the slaves for at least

300 hundred years. My method is simple. Any member of your family or your overseer can use it.

I have outlined a number of differences among the slaves, and I take these differences and make them bigger. I use distrust and envy for control purposes. These methods have worked on my modest plantation in the West Indies and it will work throughout the South. Take this simple little list of differences, and think about them. On top of my list is "Age", but it is there only because it starts with "A", the second is "Color" or shade, there is intelligence, size, sex, size of plantations, status on plantations, attitude of owners, whether the slaves live in the valley, on a hill, East, West, North, South, have fine hair, coarse hair, or is tall or short.

Now that you have a list of differences, I shall give you an outline of action, but before that, I shall assure you that distrust is stronger than trust, and envy is stronger than adulation, respect or admiration. The Black slave after receiving this introduction shall carry on and will become self refueling and self-generating for hundreds of years, maybe thousands.
Don't forget you must pitch the old Black male vs. the young Black male, and the young Black male against the old Black male.

You must use the dark skin vs. the light skin slaves, and the light skin slaves vs. the dark skin slaves.

You must use the female vs. the male, and the male vs. the female. You must also have your white servants and overseers distrust all Blacks, but it is necessary that your slaves trust and depend on us. They must love, respect and trust only us. Gentlemen, these kits are your keys to control.

Use them. Have your wives and children use them, never miss an opportunity. Used intensely for one year, the slaves themselves will remain perpetually distrustful.

Thank you gentlemen

Let's Make a Slave

It was the interest and business of slave holders to study human nature, and the slave nature in particular, with a view to practical results. I and many of them attained astonishing proficiency in this direction. They had to deal not with earth, wood and stone, but with men and by every regard they had for their own safety and prosperity they needed to know the material on which they were to work. Conscious of the injustice and wrong they were every hour perpetuating and knowing what they themselves would do. Were they the victims of such wrongs? They were constantly looking for the first signs of the dreaded retribution. They watched, therefore with skilled and practiced eyes, and learned to read with great accuracy, the state of mind and heart of the slave, through his sable face. Unusual sobriety, apparent abstractions, sullenness and indifference indeed, any mood out of the common was afforded ground for suspicion and inquiry.

Let us make a slave. What do we need? First of all we need a black nigger man, a pregnant nigger woman and her baby nigger boy. Second, we will use the same basic principle that we use in breaking a horse, combined with some more sustaining factors. What we do with horses is that we break them from one form of life to another that is we reduce them from their natural state in nature. Whereas nature provides them with the natural capacity to take care of their offspring, we break that natural string of independence from them and thereby create a dependency status, so that we may be able to get from them useful production for our business and pleasure

Cardinal Principles for making a Negro

For fear that our future Generations may not understand the principles of breaking both of the beast together, the nigger and the horse. We understand that short range planning economics results in periodic economic chaos; so that to avoid turmoil in the economy, it requires us to have breath and depth in long range comprehensive planning, articulating both skill sharp perceptions. We lay down the following principles for long range comprehensive economic planning. Both horse and niggers is no good to the economy in the wild or natural state. Both must be broken and tied together for orderly production. For orderly future, special and particular attention must be paid to the female and the youngest offspring. Both must be crossbred to produce a variety and division of labor. Both must be taught to respond to a peculiar new language. Psychological and physical instruction of containment must be created for both. We hold the six cardinal principles as truth to be self evident, based upon the following the discourse concerning the economics of breaking and tying the horse and the nigger together, all inclusive of the six principles laid down about. NOTE: Neither principle alone will suffice for good economics. All principles must be employed for orderly good of the nation. Accordingly, both a wild horse and a wild or nature nigger is dangerous even if captured, for they will have the tendency to seek their customary freedom, and in doing so, might kill you in your sleep. You cannot rest. They sleep while you are awake, and are awake while you are asleep. They are dangerous near the family house and it requires too much labor to watch them away from the house. Above all, you cannot get them to work in this natural state. Hence both the horse and the nigger must be broken; that is breaking them from one form of mental life to another. Keep the body take the mind! In other words break the will to resist. Now the breaking process is the same for both the horse and the nigger, only slightly varying in degrees. But as we said before, there is an art in long range economic planning. You must keep your eye and thoughts on the female and the offspring of the horse and the nigger. A brief discourse in offspring development will shed light on the key to sound economic principles. Pay little attention to the generation of original breaking, but concentrate on future generations.

Therefore, if you break the female mother, she will break the offspring in its early years of development and when the offspring is old enough to work, she will deliver it up to you, for her normal female protective tendencies will have been lost in the original breaking process. For example take the case of the wild stud horse, a female horse and an already infant horse and compare the breaking process with two captured nigger males in their natural state, a pregnant nigger woman with her infant offspring. Take the stud horse, break him for limited containment.

Completely break the female horse until she becomes very gentle, whereas you or anybody can ride her in her comfort. Breed the mare and the stud until you have the desired offspring. Then you can turn the stud to freedom until you need him again. Train the female horse where by she will eat out of your hand, and she will in turn train the infant horse to eat out of your hand also. When it comes to breaking the uncivilized nigger, use the same process, but vary the degree and step up the pressure, so as to do a complete reversal of the mind. Take the meanest and most restless nigger, strip him of his clothes in front of the remaining male niggers, the female, and the nigger infant, tar and feather him, tie each leg to a different horse faced in opposite directions, set him a fire and beat both horses to pull him apart in front of the remaining nigger. The next step is to take a bull whip and beat the remaining nigger male to the point of death, in front of the female and the infant. Don't kill him, but put the fear of God in him, for he can be useful for future breeding.

The Breaking Process of the African Woman

Take the female and run a series of tests on her to see if she will submit to your desires willingly. Test her in every way, because she is the most important factor for good economics. If she shows any sign of resistance in submitting completely to your will, do not hesitate to use the bull whip on her to extract that last bit of resistance out of her. Take care not to kill her, for in doing so, you spoil good economic. When in complete submission, she will train her off springs in the early years to submit to labor when the become of age. Understanding is the best thing. Therefore, we shall go deeper into this area of the subject matter concerning what we have produced here in this breaking process of the female nigger. We have reversed the relationship in her natural uncivilized state she would have a strong dependency on the uncivilized nigger male, and she would have a limited protective tendency toward her independent male offspring and would raise male off springs to be dependent like her. Nature had provided for this type of balance. We reversed nature by burning and pulling a civilized nigger apart and bull whipping the other to the point of death, all in her presence. By her being left alone, unprotected, with the male image destroyed, the ordeal caused her to move from her psychological dependent state to a frozen independent state. In this frozen psychological state of independence, she will raise her male and female offspring in reversed roles.

For fear of the young males life she will psychologically train him to be mentally weak and dependent, but physically strong. Because she has become psychologically independent, she will train her female off springs to be psychological independent. What have you got? You've got the nigger women out front and the nigger man behind and scared. This is a perfect situation of sound sleep and economic. Before the breaking process, we had to be alertly on guard at all times.

Now we can sleep soundly, for out of frozen fear his woman stands guard for us. He cannot get past her early slave molding process. He is a good tool, now ready to be tied to the horse at a tender age. By the time a nigger boy reaches the age of sixteen, he is soundly broken in and ready for a long life of sound and efficient work and the reproduction of a unit of good labor force. Continually through the breaking of uncivilized savage nigger, by throwing the nigger female savage into a frozen psychological state of independence, by killing of the protective male image, and by creating a submissive dependent mind of the nigger male slave, we have created an orbiting cycle that turns on its own axis forever, unless a phenomenon occurs and re shifts the position of the male and female slaves. We show what we mean by example. Take the case of the two economic slave units and examine them closely.

The Nigger Marriage

We breed two nigger males with two nigger females. Then we take the nigger males away from them and keep them moving and working. Say one nigger female bears a nigger female and the other bears a nigger male. Both nigger females being without influence of the nigger male image, frozen with an independent psychology, will raise their offspring into reverse positions. The one with the female offspring will teach her to be like herself, independent and negotiable (we negotiate with her, through her, by her, we negotiate her at will). The one with the nigger male offspring, she being frozen with a subconscious fear for his life, will raise him to be mentally dependent and weak, but physically strong, in other words, body over mind. Now in a few years when these two offspring's become fertile for early reproduction we will mate and breed them and continue the cycle. That is good, sound, and long range comprehensive planning.

Warning: Possible Interloping Negatives

Earlier we talked about the non economic good of the horse and the nigger in their wild or natural state; we talked out the principle of breaking and tying them together for orderly production. Furthermore, we talked about paying particular attention to the female savage and her offspring for orderly future planning, then more recently we stated that, by reversing the positions of the male and female savages, we created an orbiting cycle that turns on its own axis forever unless a phenomenon occurred and resift and positions of the male and female savages. Our experts warned us about the possibility of this phenomenon occurring, for they say that the mind has a strong drive to correct and re-correct itself over a period of time if I can touch some substantial original historical base, and they advised us that the best way to deal with the phenomenon is to shave off the brute's mental history and create a multiplicity of phenomena of illusions, so that each illusion will twirl in its own orbit, something similar to floating balls in a vacuum.

This creation of multiplicity of phenomena of illusions entails the principle of crossbreeding the nigger and the horse as we stated above, the purpose of which is to create a diversified division of labor thereby creating different levels of labor and different values of illusion at each connecting level of labor. The results of which is the severance of the points of original beginnings for each sphere illusion. Since we feel that the subject matter may get more complicated as we proceed in laying down our economic plan concerning the purpose, reason and effect of crossbreeding horses and nigger, we shall lay down the following definition terms for future generations.

Orbiting cycle means a thing turning in a given path. Axis means upon which or around which a body turns. Phenomenon means something beyond ordinary conception and inspires awe and wonder. Multiplicity means a great number. Sphere means a globe. Cross breeding a horse means taking a horse and breeding it with an ass and you get a dumb backward ass long headed mule that is not reproductive nor productive by itself.

Crossbreeding niggers mean taking so many drops of good white blood and putting them into as many nigger women as possible, varying the drops by the various tone that you want, and then letting them breed with each other until another cycle of color appears as you desire. What this means is this; Put the niggers and the horse in a breeding pot, mix some assess and some good white blood and what do you get? You got a multiplicity of colors of ass backward, unusual niggers, running, tied to a backward ass long headed mule, the one productive of itself, the other sterile. (The one constant, the other dying, we keep the nigger constant for we may replace the mules for another tool) both mule and nigger tied to each other, neither knowing where the other came from and neither productive for itself, nor without each other.

The Free Mind Paradigm

Self-Acceptance

Self-Responsibility

FREE

Respect for Free Will

FREEDOM IS IN THE MIND

The Willie Lynch Letter, regardless of whether it even actually was written by a man named Willie Lynch, provides us insight into the most powerful form of slavery. This most powerful of slavery is slavery of the mind. It stands to reason that the reversal of the process, to the extent possible, must begin there. In order for me to begin my journey toward freedom, I had to start with the freeing of my mind.

"Emancipate yourselves from mental slavery.
None but ourselves can free our minds."
— Bob Marley

The methods mentioned by Willie Lynch are sound in terms of creating a mental, and thus physical, slave. Mental slavery is in direct correlation with financial slavery. The entire process that was described in the letter was specifically designed to do three things; lower the self esteem of the slave, destroy the slave's understanding of self responsibility, and to remove the slave's awareness of the respect for free will. If this is done successfully, the master can obliterate any semblance of self completeness effectively creating a good slave to do his bidding.

Three important Tenets for the Freeing of the Mind

There are three very important tenets which aided in my journey toward freedom. They are; self acceptance, self responsibility, and respect for free will. Gaining a more clear understanding in each of these areas gave me a more clear overall perspective of the world in which we live. By making observations in each of these areas and then by implementing the lessons learned, my life began to improve substantially. You can focus on each of them to see where and how you can increase your level of freedom.

Self Acceptance

Self-acceptance can be defined in the following three ways:

• the awareness of one's strengths and weaknesses
• the realistic (yet subjective) appraisal of one's talents, capabilities, and general worth
• feelings of satisfaction with one's self despite deficiencies and regardless of past behaviors and choices.

Each of these viewpoints can have a significant impact on the level of freedom that you enjoy in your life. The primary way in which each can work against you is by the lowering of your self esteem. It's not unusual for people to compare themselves with others around them, and to feel superior or inferior towards them based on their strengths and their weaknesses. Self Esteem can also be severely impacted by years and years of conditioning leading one to have biases against themselves that they don't even know that they have, on a conscious level. How does this contribute to your enslavement? Simple, you are more apt to accept that condition as "just the way it is" or "that's the way it's always been". In addition, the way in which you view yourself has a massive effect on the way you move through this world in relation to money. As discussed many time before…slavery is all about the money.

The term "self esteem" in and of itself can be a bit misleading. Perhaps, a better way to look at it would be by using the term "them esteem". After all, in many cases, individuals with low self esteem are usually basing their self worth and self satisfaction on someone else's either real or perceived view of them. They base it on "them", some type of external evaluation rather than one originating from and determined by themselves.

Throughout history, a common way for someone to end up in the condition that we tend to think of when thinking about slavery was through debt. In most cases, too much debt is a result of too much spending. Of course, there are situations in which it seems that a sudden change of fate is the culprit. Even then, if we take a close look at the overall situation, we'll discover that there wasn't enough money to be had due to a lack of savings and investments. And, this is usually due to, that's right, overspending based on a need to overcome some condition arising from low self esteem.

Self Responsibility

There was a quote that has often been attributed to the comic book character Peter Parker's (Spiderman) uncle, Uncle Ben, "With great power comes great responsibility". If that is true, the opposite must be true as well, "With great responsibility comes great power". I don't believe that many people see it that way. In fact, if the modern state of the United States is any indication, the masses do not realize that as they give away their responsibilities…they give away their power at the same time.

Let's take a look at how that applies in terms of freedom. If we, as a society follow the path of thinking that involves handing over the responsibility of providing the populace with certain goods and services to the government, we must accept that in order for the government to provide those goods and render those services, it must have the power to do so. A mentioned earlier, one meaning of emancipation is to free from restraint, control, or the power of another. When we transfer responsibility to an external authority, we are (in fact) empowering them to use restraint (restrictions and penalties), granting them control (laws and regulations), and giving them the power (military and police) over us.

Responsibility:A detachable burden easily shifted to the shoulders of God, Fate, Fortune, Luck or one's neighbor. In the days of astrology it was customary to unload it upon a star.

- Ambrose Bierce, The Devil's Dictionary, 1911

You are responsible for the world that you live in. It is not the government's responsibility. It is not your school's or your social club's or your church's or your neighbor's or your fellow citizen's. It is yours, utterly and singularly yours.

- August Wilson

Another important aspect of self responsibility is understanding how that concept should apply to others. Just as you should hold yourself responsible for those things that you can and should do for yourself, you should hold others responsible for doing those things that they can and should do for themselves. In order to develop a free mind you must realize that self responsibility is a two-way street. By taking responsibility for yourself and your actions you become more free. By allowing others to take responsibility for themselves and their actions you become more free.

Respect for Free Will

Free will is defined as the power of acting without the constraint of necessity or fate; the ability to act at one's own discretion. Basically, this means that, in humans, it is the power or capacity to choose among alternatives or to act in certain situations independently of natural, social, or divine restraints. We've seen how racial differences have been a mechanism for determining the denial of a person's ability to exercise free will. We've also seen how social status has been used as a determining factor as well. I'm sure that some of the previous examples regarding religion and slavery make the "divine restraints" apparent .Free will is denied by some proponents of determinism.

It is true that one of the greatest sources of anger is the inability to control another adult human being. Often, when we find that we cannot impose our will on others, we become angry. The same is true of others when attempting to impose their will on us. In either case, it is an attempt to control something that cannot be controlled but rather it can only be managed. By choosing to manage these situations and interactions instead of trying to control them, we become more free.

Adding to the difficulty in grasping the concept of the respect for free will, in many cases, is the idea of the "win-lose" relationship. It is a common perception that for one to win, an other must lose. This can be clearly seen in a typical slave vs. master scenario. In order for one to benefit to the maximum extent possible, they feel the need to (and even justification for) taking advantage of another to the maximum extent possible. In order to free the mind, one must be able to shift from the win-lose mindset to a "win-win" mindset, in terms of their interaction with other human beings.

Here are some additional ways that we can show respect for free will:

We can understand that human differences are inevitable, and this is the way that it should be. Diversity is desirable and not something to be avoided or used to penalize others. It adds a fresh aspect to things and en- courages growth.

We can accept people for who they are instead of for what they believe (don't be judgmental). If you cannot accept someone for who he or she is, then you don't remain in a relationship with him or her (regardless of who it is).

We can have realistic expectations of others, not too high, not too low. And, we can remember that people (for the most part) do the best they can given their current level of knowledge and experience.

We can refrain from considering ourselves to be any better than others, but also no worse. We were all created equal regardless of cultural conditioning and there is no one class of people better or worse than another class.

We can understand that everyone is entitled to the same good things in life—no more, no less.

We can refrain from taking ourselves too seriously and keep ourselves in perspective.

We can be mindful of and respect other's rights and boundaries.

We can refrain from taking advantage of others by fostering win-win relationships.

As human beings, we are endowed with the power of choice. Understanding and exercising free will is an essential factor in separating true choice from the illusion of choice. Respecting the free will of others and demanding that they respect our free will we can place ourselves in position to better manage our interactions rather than trying to control them. They are a whole host of things we can do to demonstrate that respect for free will. Each of them moves us toward becoming more free and further away from mental slavery.

Man, Money, or the System (an attitude adjustment)

If you were to really think about it, the two elements that make slavery, in the broader sense, a reality are the presence of a society and the concept of ownership. Societies construct patterns of behavior by deeming certain actions or speech as acceptable or unacceptable. These patterns of behavior within a given society are known as societal norms. Social norms are regarded as collective representations of acceptable group conduct as well as individual perceptions of particular group conduct. They can be viewed as cultural products (including values, customs, and traditions) which represent individuals' basic knowledge of what others do and think that they should do. Ownership is the state or fact of exclusive rights and control over property, which may be an object, land or real estate, or intellectual property.

So, when given a society in which the concept of ownership prevails, it's not that far a leap for that concept to extend to the acceptable ownership of another human being. What's even more interesting is that the ownership of the person is not even necessary to create a slave like condition as it is own necessary to own the things that the other person needs. The result is a condition in which individuals are compelled to do things that they otherwise would not (free will) to meet their basic human needs... due to the constraints place on them by societal system.

This concept could be illustrated using a scale. For the purposes of this writing, we will refer to this scale as the freedom scale. It could also be referred to as the slavery scale. It demonstrates the various forms of slavery both seen and unseen. As such, it demonstrates the various levels of freedom and their indicators.

Ruled by man

Rule by man is the purest and most direct form of slavery. This is the form of slavery that we have grown accustomed to thinking about when we hear the word spoken aloud. Of course, as mentioned before, even this form is incremental in its manifestation. We can see examples of brute force and harsh treatment in some cases. In other cases we see less force applied and the treatment of the slave appearing much like that of the treatment of the average citizen. In America, an example of the contrast can be seen in the difference of treatment between the field negro and the house negro. Both were treated differently with different levels of brutality applied and differing levels of freedom but both were slaves nonetheless. In less obvious cases, the rule by man is not seen as "slavery" at all. In this day and age, if someone were to call a man your master, there would probably be a fight. Yet, most of us don't think twice about someone being called our boss.

Ruled by money

They say that money makes the world go round. As previously mentioned, debt can be defined as that state when something (usually money) is owed by one party who is called the debtor or borrower to another party who is called the creditor or lender. It can be further defined as a deferred payment, or series of payments, that is owed in the future. We can become subject to the rule of money in one of two ways. First, we can be subject by the need of it as would be the case when we simply do not earn enough or (just enough) to provide for our basic needs. Second, we can become subject to the rule of money by overspending the money that we do earn and creating debt. This debt can then become the basis for enslavement which then creates a situation which can be called debt bondage, debt slavery, or bonded labor.

One definition of the term bondage is: the state of being a slave.

Ruled by the system

No matter which way we turn, there is no escaping the system in which we live. It is a world-wide system spanning the whole of the earth and compelling all who live upon it to participate in it in some form or another whether they want to or not. This is the point in which some reading this might say, "Ha! There is no choice! This is one situation where a person cannot choose!" To that, I would respond that there is always a choice, even in this. Unfortunately, the choice that would completely extricated a person from this system is death. The system exercises control through at least three major mechanisms; Money, Religion, and Politics.

There have been many attempts to argue or reason that one can operate outside of this system. The sovereign citizen movement is one such case. It is a loose grouping of American and Commonwealth litigants, commentators, tax protesters, and financial-scheme promoters. Self-described "sovereign citizens" see themselves as answerable only to their particular interpretation of the common law and as not subject to any government statutes or proceedings. In America, many members of the sovereign citizen movement believe that the United States government is illegitimate. The Federal Bureau of Investigation (FBI) classifies some sovereign citizens ("sovereign citizen extremists") as domestic terrorists. Individuals have tried to use "sovereign citizen" arguments in U.S. federal tax cases since the 1970s. In view of such cases, the IRS has added "free born" or "sovereign" citizenship to its list of frivolous claims that may result in a $5,000 penalty when used as the basis for an inaccurate tax return.

To the extreme right of the rule by the system is the most freedom that a person can attain while still functioning as a member of a society which recognizes individual ownership. This level of freedom is achieved by conscious participation in the system and acting as the "master of your plantation". What exactly does this mean? It means that to be free we must accept that we can 't ever be "free of" the system. We must understand how the system works. We must understand how we can work within the system. We must know the rules. If we can do that and approach life with a free mind, we can make those rules work for us...and even bend a few to our will.

In the past the rule of man was established by force. This force was expressed through the whip. The whip compelled men to move as the master willed. Man was once constrained with chains. In modern times, man is constrained by increasing regulations. For the most part, the whips and chains have gone away. What remains in their stead are choices. The more choices that we have, the more freedom we can exercise. Money, no doubt, in sufficient quantities would go a long way toward providing us with more choices.

2 things...

Any slave that ever became free of his or her own volition did so by doing two things; being willing to take action and by being willing to stake their very life on the outcome.

-Dr Sherman D Rivers Sr, PhD

www.ingramcontent.com/pod-product-compliance
Lightning Source LLC
Chambersburg PA
CBHW070329220526
45467CB00001B/95